T0095458

Dewey Olmstead

LINE
UPON
LINE

*Papers from Heaven,
Messages from our Father to
help us be the best we can be*

iUniverse, Inc.
Bloomington

Line Upon Line
Papers from Heaven, Messages from our Father to help us be the best we can be

iUniverse books may be ordered through booksellers or by contacting:

iUniverse
1663 Liberty Drive
Bloomington, IN 47403
www.iuniverse.com
1-800-Authors (1-800-288-4677)

ISBN: 978-1-4697-3484-2 (sc)
ISBN: 978-1-4697-3485-9 (hc)
ISBN: 978-1-4697-3483-5 (e)

Printed in the United States of America

iUniverse rev. date: 1/24/2012

I dedicate this work to my wonderful Father in Heaven, his son Jesus Christ, my beautiful Sweetheart, all my Children, their children, their children's children, and my puppy dog, none of which I can do without.

INDEX OF PAPERS/ESSAYS

Page:	Title:	Date Written	Subject:
1	Introduction	12-Dec-11	My Story
7	Advancing Culture	1983	Progress
9	God's Creation	15-Nov-08	Amazing
11	The Plan	28-Sep-08	The Outline for Life
22	To All My Brothers and Sisters	18-Dec-08	God's Family
26	My Inheritance	29-Oct-10	Gifts Earned
31	The Word	8-Jul-06	Simple Complexity
33	One Day Many Years Ago	17-Jul-08	Hope
39	The Ark	15-Dec-06	Huge Undertaking
42	Most Religions	18-Apr-09	Only One Can Be Correct
46	Mysteries? - Not!	29-May-09	Fountain of Knowledge
51	What Can We Learn from the Scriptures?	9-Dec-07	Hidden Truths
54	Who is Your God?	22-Sep-09	Know Him
58	How Good Are You	12-Dec-09	Where Are You Going
62	So What?	2-Jul-09	Preferences
65	Choice	9-Nov-08	Ours to Use
70	Principles and Ordinances of His Church	18-Feb-08	The Law
75	According to the Law	20-Feb-10	Rules to Live by
85	One of God's Laws	14-May-03	The Rule
88	God's Laws Are Eternal	20-Feb-10	Never Changing
94	Investing in Life	20-Oct-09	Eternal Marriage
97	Are You Full of Energy?	5-Jan-11	More than you know
103	Are You Perfect?	24-Jul-09	Perfection Achieved
106	Are You Afraid?	7-Jan-10	Stay Strong, and Fear Not
109	Are You Good Enough?	8-Nov-11	Where do you Fit
113	Abraham	2-Feb-10	Sacrifice and Obedience
116	Direct Quote from the Scriptures	Long Ago	Correct Truths
120	The Book of Moses	6-Aug-09	Restoration of Lost Truths
125	Conclusion	14-Dec-11	More to Come

INTRODUCTION

I was 10 years old when my dad died. He had been sick for a long time, and mostly bed ridden for two years before he finally gave up, so I never really got to know him very well. We were not a religious family and I knew very little about religion, but before he got so sick, my dad wanted the family to be baptized, thinking it was the right thing to do. So it was arranged that the minister should come to the house and sprinkle everybody with water.

Up to that point, I might have gone to a church maybe a handful of times. So that was about all I knew about such matters, except that at the funeral I had the feeling I would see my dad again, and couldn't understand why people were so terribly depressed at his leaving.

I wouldn't say I was a dumb kid, but I sure didn't know much about that sort of thing back then.

I don't believe we had any insurance, but the good gentleman, who was the head of the company where my dad had worked, paid for him to go to the Mayo clinic in Minnesota when he started getting so horribly sick, to see if there was anything they could do for him. I believe by then, the local doctors had finally determined that what he had was something called cancer. Of course by then there was nothing they could do for him, not that knowing what it was any earlier would have helped, but they essentially sent him home to die, which turned out to be a long torturous ordeal for him.

Because there was no income to be had, my mother took in washings and ironings to make a living for herself, my sister and me. She used her old washer with the attached wringer to squeeze out the water after each of the three tubs of rinse water, and then hung them out on the clothes line to dry. When they were dry she would bring them in, iron everything neatly and then let her customers know they could come pick them up. She did an excellent job and was praised for her ability to so neatly iron the young ladies pretty ruffled dresses that were so popular at the time.

Considering she was small and less than five feet tall, it was a struggle for her I'm sure, and a very tiring and never ending chore. So before the year was over I talked the newspaper into giving me a job delivering the daily newspapers so I could have some spending money of my own and help out with expenses.

They normally required boys to be at least twelve years old before they would hire them, but under the circumstances they bent the rules for this ten year old. For one thing, it happened to be the longest route with the fewest customers per mile they had, so I don't think they could get anybody else to take it. And probably thinking I would soon give up, and then they wouldn't have to worry about it. The route was roughly seven miles long over semi rural country, and without a bike it pretty much kept me busy and out of trouble.

Fortunately it wasn't uphill both ways as some might want to tell, but it was long and tiring, especially in the winter time, when I was often trudging through snow that could be knee deep or more. Finally I inherited my sister's (girl's) bike, and that helped me get an additional route to add to the first one, giving me more customers and a little more income.

Apparently they thought I did a good enough job, because by the time I was fifteen, I had been promoted to be the circulation manager over all the other paper carriers. That meant many new things to do and a little more income. But it also required, among other things, that if one of the boys didn't get a paper to a customer, I would have to be the one to take it to them no matter where in town it might be.

Because I wasn't old enough to get a driver's license to drive, and didn't have a vehicle anyway, I had another idea. With the help of my mom I was able to get a Whizzer Motor Bike, which was like a heavy duty bicycle with a gasoline motor, or a light frame motorcycle. It would still require a driver's license to use, but I was able to talk them into giving me a restricted license for use only with a motorcycle. That worked out well. Actually I bought my first car, a 1938 Chevrolet sedan for $150 before I turned old enough to get a license to drive it, but I didn't push to get a license for that.

The real story I want to tell though, also started when I was ten years old.

Soon after my dad died, I began to realize there were things I didn't understand. Believing there had to be answers in the Bible about that sort of thing, I started reading the scriptures. It didn't seem to take long to discover that what little I knew about the church I had been baptized into was considerably different than what the Bible indicated the Lord's church was supposed to be like. That was the beginning of my search for a church that taught what the Lord said it should be.

Over the next several years I searched through, and investigated a considerable number of different denominations, always looking for the one that matched what the Bible described as being the correct way of doing things. What I found was that they each had some things that were correct, but they all came short. None of them that I looked at, which was quite a bunch, had everything they should have had according to the scriptures.

In fact by then I had decided they were **all** wrong, all of them. So I felt rather than trying to fit into something that I could see was wrong, I would come closer to being right by using the outdoors and the mountains I loved as my chapel where I could commune with God directly.

When I was twenty and decided I wanted to get married, I told my Sweetheart that I would not marry her in a church, because I felt they were all - well, I guess hypocrites - essentially teaching things that were wrong or false. My mother-in-law-to-be said she would pay for everything if we would have a church wedding - in any church I wanted. But I stood my ground and said No! I believed a Justice of the Peace had just as much authority, if not more, to do what needed to be done as any minister.

And so, we ended up being married in the in-law's living room by a Justice of the Peace, with my mom, and her dad as witnesses.

Then, several years later, now with two children already, and after moving to northern Arizona for a job with the company I had been working for, we had some neighbors who wanted to know about a church another neighbor was going to, and we were asked if we would like to also go see what it was all about. I had never heard of this church before, that I remembered, it wasn't one I had ever checked out, but I really wasn't at all interested in doing that.

My Sweetheart, however, had been wanting to go to a church, so she was interested, and kept asking me if we could just go see about it. After a bit of prolonged gentle prodding, I finally consented, with the idea that - OK, I'll go see what is wrong with this one.

There were two young fellows who came to talk to us about their beliefs and explain why they believed that way. I was ready with a ton of questions for them. Interestingly, they had the right answers according to what the scriptures had told me, for all the questions I asked.

We went back a week later. I had more questions, they had more right answers. This kept up each week, and if they didn't have an answer to one of my questions, they didn't try to fake it, they'd just say so. What they did say was they didn't know, but they would find out. The next week they came with the answers, and they were always right too.

Our just "going to find out about it", turned into many weeks of matching up right answers to all the questions I could throw at them. I don't remember for sure how long this lasted, but it was well over a year.

Finally, they asked if we wanted to be baptized. I told them I had already been baptized, but as they had explained, if it hadn't been done properly with the proper authority, it wasn't valid. I could understand that, but I told them I still had so many more questions. They told me, essentially, we would always have questions because there was more to the gospel than anyone on earth had knowledge to answer - but if we were baptized, then we would receive the gift of the Holy Ghost, who would then be our constant companion and knew all things, and He would be able to answer all of my questions.

My mind said; if this isn't the right thing to do, it won't make any difference. I would still be in the same place I was to begin with. Nothing would change, and I'd still have what I've always had. – But if it is the right thing to do, then I would be going the right direction, and that's what I wanted – so it might be worth a try.

We were baptized in a large reservoir in the middle of that high desert, one beautiful spring day, and I have never regretted my decision.

I have learned far more since that time than I could have ever imagined, and I know there are still many wonderful and amazing things yet to come for all of us to learn.

Every one of the different sections of the scriptures proves the truth of the others. They also all relate to the whole, and none of them are complete within themselves. Hopefully there will be many more sections added when all the other Tribes of Israel return home, and our Lord and Savior returns again.

This is all His world. All things are His. He will eventually win the battle over Satan, and that evil serpent will be sealed away permanently to his fate.

I invite everyone to come with me into the incredible world of God's Kingdom where we can all receive His marvelous blessings.

A note of explanation: The papers and pages that follow are bits of what I call wisdom from God. They are not necessarily my thoughts. They came from someone on high that knows more about these things than I do. Like the light bulb that lights over your head with information you might need to solve a problem, or tell you something you need to know. I only tried to write them down in my own clumsy and sometimes awkward way to try to get the point across.

Most of them seemed to come to fill a need, or help someone comprehend something they didn't understand - or had questions about - or that I saw they could use - or needed to understand.

They might have come for a certain someone, but with the potential to enlighten many others. That is why I finally decided I needed to put them into a book so they could be shared with a wider audience. They even helped me understand things better. So that is my wish and hope; that many, many people will discover this book and find something of worth that they can use to better their lives.

One thing you need to understand. These papers are not necessarily related to each other. In other words, you don't read this like a normal book expecting one chapter to follow another. If you notice, the dates when they were written vary considerably, and bounce all over. So do the ideas. But they all relate to the truths that are in the scriptures, and the true gospel of Jesus Christ.

Each paper is usually quite short and they can each be read all by themselves for a quick bite of inspiration, and might even be more beneficial if approached separately that way. This is not a complete work, so don't get the impression anything said here is the final or complete word on the subject. However, if a thought doesn't seem to be complete, and give you the answer you might be looking for, it might be intended that way to encourage you to seek out the answers in the scriptures that fit your situation.

You *need* to read, **must** read, and reread, the scriptures to constantly discover new things, and the answers you need for yourself - in your particular moment. You shouldn't even depend on what I tell you, other than to use it to start your mind moving, hopefully, in the right direction, toward your Father in Heaven, His Son Jesus Christ, and the Holy Ghost. Please search the scriptures for yourself.

Any words you might be unfamiliar with, like testament, covenant, ordinance, scripture, Holy Ghost, etc. are not defined here, since this isn't that type of reference work, they should be able to be found in a good Bible Dictionary. But I believe everything is scripturally correct, although with my own slant on how it is presented, and in my own sort of down-home way. Other than that, they essentially all relate to the scriptures and the truths that can found there. And which can probably also be learned from inspiring thoughts from the Holy Ghost.

I don't guarantee my prose to be correct (or what **you** need) will be answered here, but if not, I hope you can forgive me for my literary errors, and use these things as that primer to help you search and find the scriptures you need to learn from.

If you have questions, there are probably answers in the scriptures, or the answers can be received from the Holy Ghost if you petition him in your sincere daily prayers. You as a man or woman, and child of God, can even receive the Holy Ghost as your *constant* companion. This is given by someone that holds the Holy Priesthood. And remember - don't ever be deceived by someone telling you lies. Verify for yourself, whether the things you hear, or are told, are true or false.

It is my sincere prayer that all who read these things here, will also gain the wisdom, and the salvation they seek, by diligent investigation, study, and personal growth and practice. And I say these things in the name of Jesus Christ, amen.

14-Dec-11

ADVANCING CULTURE

For thousands of years there was virtually no advancement in the culture of man, or the way life was lived. There were definitely some ups and downs over the ages, but generally speaking, there were very few major, or at least very wide spread changes, that we are aware of. Then less than 200 years ago, for reasons most people don't understand, the world began to advance and progress. As a snowball rolling down a hill swells upon itself, so has invention and technology since then. And just as particles begin to bombard their neighbors in a critical mass of Uranium 235, the activity multiplies into a massive explosion.

The industrial age has come with its organization and massive power, but now already is dwindling in the face of this new intellectual age, which is rolling in as the snowball. An age of information, of knowledge, of advancement; an age where society as a whole is not able to keep up, and even those involved in this explosion of advancements are left in the wake because other fields, and new fields, are spreading by the square of the distance in time.

We are living in this unique period of history where a new invention of yesterday is not seen today as the miracle it once was, and tomorrow it is already virtually obsolete. This is especially true in the field of electronics and the associated areas of computers and robotics. Unlike the massiveness of the industrial age however, this new age of technology is involved in the miniature and microscopic areas of reality. It almost makes you wonder – what is reality?

From computers that were massive and filled an entire room (typical of the industrial era) complex, complicated, finicky, funky, and fallible, progression has carried them to capable, compact, dependable, friendly and smart. And though there are still computer monsters, they are miniature monsters – miniature in relative size compared to previously, but monsters of capability. And even friendly. . ? Perhaps!

So friendly, you operate them with a "mouse," like on the Local Integrated Software Architecture computer, better known as "Lisa." Or smart? You can operate a Texas Instruments computer by just talking to it, using what's called "usable voice recognition." Even these things are now, at the time of *this* writing, "far in the past."

But the snowball doesn't end here. Coupled with robotics, the computer brain of these metal androids converts voice commands into physical actions.

How long until the computers fifth, sixth, or seventh generation – the computers that not only think, but reason, will be controlling the machines of the future, operating the risky, dangerous and life threatening situations without the intervention of man? Yes, they already are.

One thing is certain – "Anything the mind can conceive and believe can be achieved," (Napolean Hill) – There is a God, and we are His special creation. We were created in His image. Within each of us He has planted a seed of greatness. As the little acorn can become a giant oak, so can we mature and grow up to be "even as He is." (Moroni 7:48)

But we must care for this seed. Nourish it with the Scriptures, water it with baptism, add sunshine that comes through the Holy Ghost and the Prophets, strengthen it with the winds of struggle and trouble, germinate it with Temple ordinances, and someday we will be as the giant oak – even as our Heavenly Father *is*. We are His seed and He has given us the potential to be "even as I am." (D&C 29:12) Now is the time to prepare.

What are we going to do with it?

1983

GOD'S CREATION

There are 12 Inches in 1 Foot
There are 5,280 Feet in 1 Mile
The Missouri River is 2,540 Miles Long
It takes "Light" less than 0.014 of a ***second*** to travel that 2,540 miles
Light Travels 186,000 Miles in 1 Second
That is 11,160,000 Miles in 1 Minute
That is 669,600,000 Miles in 1 Hour
That is 16,070,400,000 Miles in 1 Day
That is 5,865,696,000,000 Miles in 1 Year - This is the ***distance*** of one ***"Light Year"***
If light traveled in a straight line, for 1 year, this is how far it would go in that time.

The next star nearest to our Sun, is Alpha Centauri, which is 23,462,784,000,000 miles away, so if you could travel at 669,600,000 miles per hour (the speed of light), it would take at least 4 years to get there – if you didn't make any pit-stops!

Our Milky Way Galaxy is approximately 586,569,600,000,000,000 miles across from one edge to the other, so if you could travel at the Speed of Light (186,000 Miles per Second), it would take you approximately 100,000 ***Years*** to get from one edge to the other - (Again, with no pit-stops.)

The next galaxy nearest our Milky Way Galaxy, is the Andromeda Galaxy, it is only about 12,904,531,200,000,000,000 miles away. That means it would take you 2,200,000 *Years* to get there – going at the speed of Light!

Our whole Solar System is only a tiny, tiny speck in our little Milky Way Galaxy, and there are hundreds of thousands of galaxies, some many times bigger than the little one we live in. Have you ever stopped to think how many worlds similar to ours there must be, just in our measly little galaxy? God told the Prophet Moses, 1:33 *"worlds without number have I created; and I also created them for mine own purpose; and by the Son I created them, which is mine Only Begotten. But only an account of this earth, and the inhabitants thereof, give I unto you. For behold, there are many worlds that have passed away by the word of my power. And there are many that now stand, and **innumerable** are they unto man; but all things are numbered unto me.*

   Or have you stopped to realize how infinitesimally small you are in the immensity of space? – ***But***, in spite of that, *you* are **not** insignificant or unimportant in all of this. God knows who you are. He even knows you by your given name. You are not inconsequential to him.

   If you have been brain-washed into believing you are an accident of nature, I am sorry for you. You have a brain, is that an accident? I don't think so. So use it. There is a God who put all things in motion, who set the stars in their places, and attached and linked them together with gravity, centrifugal, and other forces for a special purpose. Once you allow yourself to recognize, not only its immensity, but how and why it is all interconnected, you will begin to understand what your purpose is, and how important even *you* are.

   Don't allow the hatred of the Evil-One to destroy you and your destiny, or let anyone else keep you from achieving what God has put you here to achieve. All the beauty and majesty of this tiny rock we live on, testifies to the magnificence of God and His creation – ***including you***.

15-Nov-2008

THE PLAN

Just what is this "plan," and how does it affect me? Let's start with the basics. Do you believe there is a God? What about the Bible? Have you ever read any of the scriptures, or know anything about them? You should; they are the operation and instruction manuals for people. They contain the layout, rules and description of God's *plan.* Part of which tells you how you were made, what you need to do to keep running properly, and what kind of warrantee you have. They also define God's master plan - the reason for this earth and why we are all here. It may be hard to understand exactly what this plan is, or how it works, unless you study those scriptures.

If you have been exposed to the scriptures in any way, then you might have heard a little bit about Adam and Eve, Moses, Abraham, Isaac, Joseph and Mary, and Jesus. God created each and all of them, in fact, He created all of us, you, me, and everyone else that has ever lived, or will ever live, on this beautiful earth. But he created us spiritually first. That spirit part of us is the essence of what we are and makes us who we are. You could say that was the first step in God's marvelous plan.

So who is God? He is a man, a being, just like you and me, but that has achieved "Godhood" status because of his knowledge, his wisdom, his learning, his purity, and his goodness. He is the spiritual creator of all things, as it says in the scriptures. Not only of the earth and universe, but of every one of us, before we came to this earth. He is our Father, and we are his children. And since that place where we were created is called Heaven, he is our Heavenly Father.

That being the case, it is logical to assume we have a Heavenly Mother as well. I don't think she has ever been mentioned in the scriptures, at least I don't remember reading about her, but if we are children to a Father, it is reasonable to assume that we have a Mother as well. And I believe it is for a definite purpose that she is not mentioned. I'm sure we will learn all about her when the time is right, and we'll realize that one reason God is so great is because he has a wonderfully, smart, wise, intelligent wife (like the rest of us guys that are married.)

In that first "spiritual existence," or "pre-existence", where we came to be, we knew our Heavenly Father, and he knew each of us very well, in fact, He still knows us, each and every one of us by our own given name.

Part of *our* creation that still wasn't totally complete up to that point, involves all of us receiving bodies of flesh and bones to house our spirits and give us substance, just like our Heavenly parents have, and to make it possible for us to do everything our Father can do.

For this purpose of obtaining bodies, and testing our values, an "earth" was also created for us, along with its moon, stars, and brilliant sun to control and regulate this beautiful world we live on, so we would have a place, the chance, and the opportunity to fulfill this part of His "plan", to receive our bodies of flesh and bones.

However, as part of *"the plan,"* our memories, and intimate knowledge of our Father, were taken away temporarily for a specific purpose when we came to this earth. That's part of the testing; and why we don't remember anything else right now. And why we have to read about it in the scriptures written by special individuals, known as Prophets that have earned the right, and the ability, to talk **with** God. We all can talk **to** him any time we want; unfortunately we don't listen too well, so most of the time when he talks to us we don't hear what he has to say, or to tell us.

There are many characteristics you can attribute to God, but the first and most significant one you need to realize is that He has a greater LOVE for us (his children) than anything our tiny mortal minds can wrap around. This can't be emphasized enough. He is just the greatest parent, and example of love, there is.

Some of us have a hard time understanding that attribute in our own homes, because we don't have enough love for our parents, our spouse, our brothers and sisters, or even our children. But God's love is infinite for every one of us, even the ones that turn out to be real creeps. He doesn't like what they do, but He still loves them. That's just the way he is, and why He is God, and why He would really rather we were all honest, kind and good.

Beyond that, of course, He has more knowledge, power, and abilities, than anything we can possibly understand – especially since we don't have any of the memories anymore of that pre-existence. Those are all some of the things we need to try to learn, or perhaps relearn, while we're here on the earth.

If you can imagine yourself creating a world such as we live on, along with all its many wonders, and the associated universe that controls all its motions, influences, etc. you might just begin to understand a project of that immensity, and the knowledge He must have. I have a hard time making a good sandwich, let alone a mountain, tree, or a sun.

Another attribute He has is his dedication, and obedience, to law and order. You see, for every law there is a blessing, **and** a penalty, connected to it. He knows them all and follows every one of them precisely. If we follow these laws and do something good, we *must* receive a blessing – that is getting something good, for doing something good! It is an eternal law, and isn't it a wonderful one.

However, if we do something wrong, we must then pay a penalty. That is just part of the eternal law as well. For instance, if we stole something from somebody, or do anything else that is morally wrong, we *will* be penalized for it – that is, we **WILL** be penalized for it. We may think we're getting away with something, and maybe we will for a while and won't be caught and thrown into jail, or whatever, but eventually that penalty *will* have to be paid – that is the law. There is no escaping it; it's an eternal law, not like our wimpy earthly laws.

So how does all this fit into this "plan?"

Where God lives, is Heaven, and everything in Heaven is fine and good and that is the way it should be, and always will be. There are no creeps or scumbags there. God likes that and loves it there, and He also wants as many of his children to come back to live with him as possible, in a place like that, after they get their bodies, but He doesn't want any creeps or scumbags coming, so He wants to make sure we're worth having in His Kingdom.

So, way back then, when we were all contemplating getting our bodies, we all got together with him in a big council to decide how this should be accomplished. There would have to be a test to see who was good enough to actually live in that special place, and it would be different when we have bodies, than it had been when we were just spirits.

Two plans were submitted to Father in Heaven, and to all of us. One of the plans was that we would all **have** to do what someone says we have to do; we just wouldn't have a choice to do anything else.

But that would take away our free agency. We wouldn't have the right to choose what we wanted to do, which was one of Heaven's rights. And any creep could do that, besides, the submitter of this plan wanted every bit of the credit for keeping everything in control, usurping God of his authority. There was **no way** that was ever going to happen, so of course that was totally unacceptable.

The other plan that was submitted was that we would be given a *choice* in everything, to see if we would choose to be good, or if we wanted to be a scumbag. That meant we'd have to follow the law, all on our own. And if we chose to do *everything* right, and everything we were supposed to do, we would get to go back to live with our parents and receive **everything**. That is, we could get all the blessings and good things we could ever possibly imagine, the same as our parents, and live in that marvelous place called Heaven that was absolutely perfect.

All of us that have come to this earth to receive a body, agreed to that plan – we had a choice then to do what we wanted to do, and now we still do,.

However, if we did something wrong out of ignorance, not understanding the law, in a weak moment, etc., which was bound to happen, not knowing any more than we know – well, that could be bad, because if you remember, according to the law, doing something wrong requires that a penalty **has** to be paid, and that would also bump us out of place from getting back to that perfect place called Heaven.

But in this plan - there would be a way provided to overcome that wrong and get us back on the right path again, if we want to and did what we had to do. That sounds good, but how could that happen? I'll tell you in a bit.

I'm sure at the time, we understood what all the laws were that we needed to follow, but now without those memories, we can't remember what they all were, so some special people were called that were good enough they could commune with those "back home." And the things they learned they wrote down for us so we would know what we were supposed to do.

These special people were called Prophets because they always seemed to know so much.

A lot of those things they wrote down though were lost, however the ones we found and saved were gathered together into books that we now call the scriptures. Some of them can be really hard to read and understand, but if we do our best, we can learn a lot about God's plan and the two people who presented those two plans.

They were two very different types of individuals, and the one that wanted to *make* everyone do things his way, became very angry that his plan wasn't chosen. And he openly rebelled against our Father in Heaven, so Father threw him out of His kingdom.

Him, being the type of creep he is, vowed that if he was expelled, and had to leave, he would do everything he could to destroy any of the rest of us he could to keep us from getting back to Heaven. And I guess there were about another third of us that felt the same way.

The instigator of that ludicrous plan was named Lucifer, and those that followed him became his followers. Since then, Lucifer became the one we call Satan, the Devil, the father of corruption, lies, deceit, and all things bad. And as you probably realize, or at least should, Satan and his followers are still out there all around us doing their best to mess everybody up that they possibly can.

Because they never received bodies, and are still only spirits, we don't normally see them while we're here on the earth, but don't be fooled; they are all still out there doing their dirty work. And it gets worse all the time!

The individual that submitted the other plan is none other than the "first born" of our Father in Heaven. He goes by several other names as well, for instance we also know him as Jehovah, the Messiah, the God of the ancient world (in the Old Testament), the Savior, the Son of God, even Jesus who is the Christ. You see, he had to come to the earth just like we did so he could get his own body too.

Before he did though, he was given the assignment to give substance to all of the things God, His Father, had created spiritually. This Jesus is the one who *physically* created this world, and essentially gave physical bodies to this entire universe we live in according to God's master plan.

So, even though God created everything we know, Jesus was the one who gave it all substance. In that respect He is also the (physical) creator of the earth and everything on it; the trees, plants, birds, fowls, fishes, animals, and even the first man and woman. That is why he was known as God in olden times, and sometimes known as Father, because he was the one who *physically* created these things. Of course he is also known as the Son, because he was the only "begotten" Son of God on the earth. (That means he was literally the son of God, and not actually the son of Joseph.)

He also has "followers" that help him with his chores and duties, and of course these are the ones we usually call angels. They are on the "good" side, and sometimes those others from the bad side try to look like the good guys, so you have to really watch out for that.

And there are those others that were mentioned. They are especially good people that have come to earth to get their bodies that also have special callings to help us know what we should be doing. They are those called the Prophets, and are the ones who wrote things to put in the scriptures.

Because Jesus submitted **this** "plan," He agreed to carry out the assignment, to spell it out and define it to the Prophets who wrote them down in the scriptures for us. That way we also would have them, and know what they are, since we wouldn't remember them once we got here.

This was logical because Jesus was the one who knew the plan we accepted the best, and how it followed the law. So this is also the reason he is known as God, the giver of the law, in the Old Testament.

He is also the one who gave Moses the Ten Commandments, which were temporal laws for those who didn't seem to want to obey the spiritual laws that Moses was trying to teach them.

Those commandments are very basic laws that mainly help you

be good if you do them. They aren't all the laws, or those that will ultimately get you back into Heaven. They just prepare you for the really important ones.

There are more spiritual laws, and ordinances, that we have to follow to do that, and are the ones the Prophets are constantly trying to teach us. They are also the same laws that are in the Kingdom of Heaven, which even God obeys, and which we need to learn, to allow us to get back into Heaven and receive all those blessings and good things God has to give us.

This "plan" then, is the "Plan of Salvation". It is the whole organization of the laws, rules, and ordinances that combine to control all those who live in this vast universe, and what we must do to inherit Heaven for our eternal home.

The reason our memories were taken away from us can now be explained – If we knew all of those things that happened before we came here, they would heavily influence us. That means we wouldn't be able to freely make up our own minds the way we should, about what we think is right, and should do.

It would be like cheating on a test. We might have the right answer, but we wouldn't have learned anything. And when the time came that we had to know what we had to do that was right, we wouldn't know it. There are no short cuts to knowing what is right, and getting into Heaven. But actually, we can't get away with cheating anyway, because God knows everything you are doing, how you are thinking, and why you are doing what you are doing. You just have to prove to Him that **you** know why you're doing what you're doing.

Ultimately, if we obey all those laws and ordinances we will be able to actually live with God in his mansions (and that is what he is hoping for and wants you to do too, of your own free will and choice.). There are many things to learn, things to do, and ordinances to perform to achieve that status, but there are many "helps" as well, and we have the scriptures and Prophets to teach us, and to learn from. But we still have to do them for ourselves if we want them to count.

We don't have to learn them all at once though. We are told we can learn them step-by-step, bit-by-bit, line-upon-line, precept upon precept, here a little, there a little. Baby steps if need be, as long as we are always headed in the right direction, and always correcting our direction when we stray off the correct path. That will keep us going in the RIGHT direction.

So what are those provisions mentioned for eliminating the wrong things we've done so we can still get all that good stuff?

First of all, we should want to do things right even if we don't get any "good stuff" or reward at all. But if you still want to know, remember, since a penalty is *required* for doing something wrong, and a penalty *must* be paid, then that means someone is going to have to pay that penalty, that debt. Who is that going to be – who **can** that be, if you can't do it yourself?

This would require someone with strength, ability, faith, great love, and a spotless record without any fault – absolutely perfect.

Not only that, to do everything else that needed to be done, they would actually have to *sacrifice* their own life to show that when we die we will live again - forever. And this individual would have to do all this of their own freewill, and do all the other things in a perfect way to be worthy and capable of paying this debt. Of course he must also have had the same trials and the same difficulties in this life to overcome as we do, to know what it was all about and prove he would do everything perfectly and completely. He would also be required to complete all the ordinances we are required to do to show us the way, the right way, and what has to be done.

As you might imagine, this would be extremely difficult for many reasons. Besides, this special individual would also have to be subject to all the same evil influences mentioned above that all of us are subject to. And Satan would try even harder to corrupt and destroy this special individual, than all the rest of us combined, to thwart this "great plan." (He is just one nasty, mean, ornery cuss!)

The only individual who could do this was Jesus, the one who submitted "the good plan," he who was to become the Christ, the literal Son of God; that would *save* us from our wrongs (our sins.) This is the reason we call him our Savior, and why we call this plan the "plan of Salvation."

To help him do all the miracles and things he needed to do, he was given a very special gift, and very special earthly parents. That gift was to have a very special birth. Of course, he had to have an earthly, mortal body the same as all the rest of us, and that was why he came to earth to be born of Mary. (You know, she must have been a very special and wonderful person that apparently was almost faultless herself, to be chosen for that special privilege.) It was of course a mortal birth that allowed him to receive a body like us, and be subject to all our earthly laws, our earthly influences, temptations, etc. But he was also given the privilege of having a very special Father – who was actually God himself. That of course made him half human and half God, so He was a very special person indeed.

Now there is at least one more thing. Since this is a mortal world, and our spirits were placed into mortal bodies – when our body dies, our spirits don't have anywhere to live and have to leave, until they receive their newly renewed body back. Does that mean our spirits are out there floating around somewhere again with no place to go when that happens.

Simply, no! If we are good, God has made a place for our spirits to go where we don't have to associate with Satan and his bunch of cronies, and there we can be learning more of the things we need to know about our home in Heaven. Jesus called that place Paradise when he was talking to the one man on the cross next to him when they were crucified. Remember, Paradise is **not** Heaven – they weren't going *there* yet.

Remember too, he was not talking to the man that railed on him, but only the one who accepted him as the Christ. We have to accept this Jesus as the Christ, if we wish to receive our blessings, but that is only part of what we must do to return to **Heaven**.

This great plan of Jesus of course provided for all things. He allowed evil men to kill his mortal body so he could show us how this resurrection was to come about. And after being crucified, losing his mortal body, going to Paradise, and seeing his Heavenly Father for approval of his work on earth, he came back 3 days later. There He redeemed his body from the tomb, restored it into a living perfected eternal body for his spirit to live in, and proclaimed that everyone else who had died, or will ever die after living on this earth, even the scumbags, would also be **resurrected** (restored) into perfected bodies that would live forever – and is why we call him the Redeemer, because he redeemed us from death. (That doesn't mean the scumbags will turn into good people, it just means they will have their bodies back and still be scumbags with new bodies.)

Jesus now lives with his Father, our Father, in Heaven. We know this because the living Prophets, those who are alive in our world today, have seen them together, and he still talks to the Prophets and guides His Church through them, which essentially is the Plan of Salvation in action.

The important thing to note is that before Jesus was crucified, he went to the Garden of Gethsemane and took upon himself, all by himself, all of the penalties of every person who would ever live on this earth, and paid for them all by himself.

That was so horrible and painful for him that he actually bled from every pore of his body. He is the only one with the strength, love and purity who could have ever done that. And He had enough that He did it for all the rest of us.

But if we don't appreciate what He did for us, and accept Him as the payer of our debts, then we will have to pay for our own debts, by suffering just like He did, for all of us.

That has to give you something very serious to think about.

There is, of course, much more to this over simplification of "The Plan" than I have relayed in this short paper, but hopefully it is enough to not only give you hope, but to inspire and encourage you to learn more, and become perfect. To search the scriptures for yourself, to learn what you must do, and what you *have* to do to earn your rewards. How to be properly baptized and how to do those other ordinances that are so important to your own salvation.

It really is much simpler than most would want you to believe - but remember – **The laws of God are unbendable and unchangeable, there is no other way than the right way.** If you don't carefully follow the law, and do it according to the plan, it doesn't work. All you are doing if you don't do it right is fooling yourself, spinning your tires without going anywhere.

For your own sake, seek the right way from the scriptures and the living Prophets who are here to help and teach us those spiritual laws we need to follow, to return to live with our Father who is in Heaven waiting for us. And if you don't want to pay for your own penalties, by yourself, you better get to know Jesus Christ.

This is the Plan of Salvation in a capsule. To get the whole story, study the scriptures, listen to the Prophet and Apostles and be obedient to all His laws, and you'll never have to look back, you'll have the assurance of knowing what is right, and if followed will lead you in an undeviating path toward Heaven where you can receive all the blessings God has for you.

If you take any other way than the one approved of God, it is unlikely you will ever get to where you want to be. At least not without some serious pain on your part and intervention by Him and others who will have to overcome the rocks you have strewn in your wake. Even then and even with help in the Temples of the Lord, you may not be able to retrieve all that may be lost if you don't start doing the right things, the right way, that you should be doing.

All these things are still true, and can be found by all who diligently seek them. I testify to their truth, and I bear this testimony to all, in the name of Jesus Christ, Amen.

28-Sep-2008

TO ALL MY BROTHERS AND SISTERS

I would guess that almost everybody has a Bible in their home. Do you read yours? Most people don't, so they don't really know what it is about, or what it says. I am not a religious fanatic, but I have read my Bible more than once and even studied it quite a bit too, so I have a pretty good understanding of what is in there – and am still learning!

I guess any Bible will do, but the King James Version, though perhaps a little more difficult to read and possibly understand, is by far much better than one that has been interpreted yet again by someone else who just wants to make it *a little easier to read*. Modifying and reinterpreting what is said there will lose some very important things that we need to learn about. Even the King James Version has already lost many plain and precious things of importance that were in the original text, so – as important as it is, you don't want to miss out on something else.

One thing about scripture, that defines it as scripture, is that no matter who reads it, or for what reason, or how many times you read it, it can give you the answers you are seeking. If someone puts their own slant on what *they* believe it says it takes away from what you can find that will specifically help you, in your time of need, when you need it the most. With that being said, what else is the Bible all about? The best way, of course, to find out is to read it yourself – you will find something (many things) in there especially for you that someone else won't ever see.

Something else you have to realize is that everything you need to know isn't in there. If it contained everything you needed to know, and spelled it out for you, it would be too big to carry and get through the door. But actually, it still contains most of what you need to know for now, and the important things are usually repeated over and over by every Prophet that has his writings in there. The rest can be gotten through prayer, and listening to the Prophets.

What it ***does*** tell you is that we are not an accident of nature. There is a Supreme Being we call "God" that created this World (and this entire Universe) especially for you (well, for every one of us, but you are just as important as any other person that has ever lived, no matter what your earthly status might be.) We are all children of this Supreme Being – we are all brothers and sisters in the family of God. And to Him you are very important.

It is hard for our feeble minds to understand how someone like him could exist, but it is the truth testified to by all the Holy Prophets that have ever lived, and by me who is writing this. I want you to understand this for your sake. Not for anyone else, just for you and your family.

There is a reason God made this world, He had a plan, and you are a part of that plan. If this was not true, there would be no reason for this world, or you. And there is also a reason why sometimes you have to struggle to live a life that at times seems to be pointless. There is a reason, and if we understand that reason, we can begin to make sense of why we are here, and can use it to our advantage. That reason might only be to help us learn what is right, but it is so much more. And remember, the knowledge we obtain in this life is the only thing we are going to take with us when we leave here.

Something else the Bible tells us is that the Christ who was born to Mary in the meridian of time, and that we celebrate at Christmas time, was born, lived, and was crucified by evil men for a very special purpose. That singular purpose was for ***you***!

So when you die, you will not actually die, only your body dies. Your spirit – the real part of what makes you you - does not die, and in time, just like Jesus Christ, your spirit will get a new perfected body, and you will live again, still, and forever. And, *provided you have done what you need to do,* you can possibly even go to live with that God who created you, just like Jesus has done after he was resurrected – if you earn that right by what you do.

The Bible also warns us of the one called Lucifer, Satan, or the Devil. Who, no matter by what name he is called, wants to bring doubt, fear and hopelessness into your mind. He wants to deceive you, lie to you, and in fact wants to destroy you so you will never be able to live with your God. The Bible tells about him; and what you need to know to keep from being dragged down to Hell by him - and with him.

Also, it tells what you need to know to earn all the fabulous rewards and gifts you can receive by being obedient to the laws of God and rising to live the life He wants you to live with Him in Heaven.

And yes, there is, and must be, opposition in all things. In other words for everything good there is something bad, and for everything bad there is something good. We need to learn that. And that is Satan's purpose; to show us that there is an opposite to everything. And those are also the things we can learn from studying the scriptures, so we don't have to listen to Satan.

But Satan cannot force us to do anything wrong. If we do something wrong, it is because we chose to do it that way. We have been given our free agency to choose for ourselves what we want, whether we want to do good things or bad. It is up to us. Just remember, when we do good things we receive rewards, and when we do bad things we must pay a penalty. Thankfully the Bible is like the owner's manual to help us know what is right, and what we must do to earn all the rewards our Heavenly Father has for us.

The Scriptures also tells us He will never forsake us if we don't forsake him. But if we do, then he has made no promise to help us either. According to them though, he does promise us that he will continue to give us more help than just what is in the five books of Moses, or in Isaiah, or Matthew, etc. He is not dead. In fact He is the same yesterday, today, ***and forever***, (Hebrews 1:10-12) He continues to help us and will continues to send his Prophets to help, teach and guide us, and continue to give us more information *as long as we don't forsake him.*

We therefore **must** keep him in our lives, in our land, in our Government, in our thoughts, and in our prayers, always thanking him for all he does (and has done for us) and for all those many blessings he freely gives to us every day. He does not lie, and keeps *all* his promises.

You, me and all of our brothers and sisters, and this world, is what the scriptures and Jesus Christ are all about. Study and learn all you can from them so you will be numbered among those who will go back to live with our Heavenly Parents who gave us all we have, and still have much, much more to give.

18-Dec-2008

MY INHERITANCE

As a child of loving, eternal, perfect parents, I have inherited amazing capabilities without limits as to what I can accomplish, or am capable of. Their love is infinite, and their desire for me to have all that they have is tempered only by their hope that I am worthy of it.

My mother is the most beautiful of any woman I could ever imagine, with smooth flawless skin and long flowing wavy hair. She has love, and kindness without limits; is warm, gentle, caring, and with deep emotions that are without measure.

My father is strong, honest, obedient, resourceful, and perfect in every way. He has no faults or weaknesses of any kind that might reduce or diminish any of his qualities. He knows exactly what is right and never deviates from that stance in the slightest degree.

They both know my abilities, and capabilities, and know that I come from pure stock with an honest desire to emulate every good quality I have seen in their example. I was created from pure, infinite materials of the highest quality, giving me the capability of perfection, and a desire to reach that same flawless perfection they have achieved in their lives, yet with the choice to choose for myself what I want to achieve. And, if I am not deceived or influenced or led astray by someone, or something, I can achieve anything I wish.

In spite of this rather perfect beginning, they know I have not yet achieved perfection. They don't know if I will hold on to those principles as I grow up if tempted by other influences.

However, they want me to have the opportunity to learn everything necessary to reach that goal of perfection, if that is my choice.

To do that, I need to be tried and even tempted to see if I will hold on to the perfect principles I have been taught. And to do that, they have removed my memory of things I've already learned to keep that from influencing me, so I can decide for myself what I want out of life. And then temporarily sent me here, to another home where conditions are less than ideal, and not very stable. But are provided to allow this testing to be accomplished, where I am forced to make my own decisions, and choices, be they right or wrong.

This is much more difficult than it might at first appear, because up to this point I have lived in a peaceful home in an environment of love, with perfect parents. Where there were no distracting wrong influences that would bring about a departure from that perfect condition I was used to. And even though I really don't remember it, I even then had the choice to choose what I wanted to do, and my choice was to come here, to be tested.

Besides that, I now have a new physical body that I am not familiar with, or used to, with capabilities I have not known before. Or do I know quite how to handle it, or the sensations associated with this new experience.

I also recognize this body has abilities I never totally understood before, and it is somewhat difficult knowing just what I can do, and still keep control of the associated emotions that seem to go along with it. I also see why it is so important to learn these things, if I want to remain a child of my perfect parents. And to be one they would want to come back home to live with them.

However, in this present home away from home, they have provided everything I really need to make the right decisions. But perhaps not everything I want – which is good, because that means there are still things I need to be striving for, and working toward.

How worthless life would be if I had everything I wanted, even though I might wish for that. Deep down inside, I understand I have the capability to get whatever I need if I just learn how to do it, but at this point, the knowledge of just how to do that has left me, along with the memories I used to have about my parents and that original home.

But understanding these things helps me realize that I have not been left all alone, and still have the capacity to grow into someone as excellent as my parents. All I need to do is search for the truth, using the scriptures and prayer; be obedient to the truth I find, and try to live according to the laws which rule this universe. Thankfully, those laws are the same laws that rule even that place from where I came.

I am of course, talking about this mortality now, and those parents, being my Heavenly Parents. That makes me a child of God. Therefore, I should have that capacity to do marvelous things, especially with the knowledge that I gain here, on my own.

Looking at it from that perspective, I have learned that my Father designed this world similar to His own, and had his *Chosen Son* construct it for us to those specifications. The major differences are that this world was all made out of temporary materials.

Evil was also introduced to tempt and try us, by providing the inverse of good, to present both sides of the picture to us. That allows us, or probably more correctly, **requires** us to choose what we want to do without the influence of our parents. This then will determine, by our own natural/inner desires and preference, what we want to do, or be. Not only here, but more importantly, what we want to be and do after we leave here.

Recognizing that the influence of evil would be so great, and "almost" over powering at times, a means was also provided to overcome the stain of that evil, once it was realized and corrected for, to allow us to be cleansed of it and returned to a more pure state. And eventually to be fully purified, if that is what we ultimately desire and work for. That would allow us to return to that pure existence that we now call Heaven, to live again as perfected souls with our Heavenly parents.

The one big question we all have in this world is; how do we obtain all those things we need and want to live properly here? Unfortunately, there are many who are willing to tell us how to do or get things, but they often aren't correct, and don't take into consideration the laws that govern what is correct. Therefore, we often wander, or are led into evil paths which lead us to destruction – if we don't wake up and learn for ourselves what the truth really is.

First of all, we need to learn (again) about our Heavenly Father, what this life is all about, and why we are here upon this mortal earth. Learn the laws that we are subject to, and must be obedient to – and to understand about evil, and why it is so adamant about opposing what is right.

For these purposes, God has assigned special witnesses, called Prophets, to lay out the many laws for us, to explain what is right and wrong, and to warn us of the consequences of not following those laws. These authorized messengers are the ones who really know the truth, and the laws governing us, because they communicate with God, and they won't lead us in the wrong direction.

These things have been written down for us over the centuries, often as examples and stories to read, to compare to ourselves, and learn from. Fortunately, some of those writings still exist. And with each new dispensation and Prophet that is called; all these things are restored again, repeated, reiterated, and/or added to as needed and necessary, for us to learn and grow from.

Then we need to go to work, put all we learn to good use, and perhaps even continue to learn and struggle with the burdens that might be placed upon our backs to test us. It can be hard as we study and learn every law and what we need to do to fulfill each one. But we were never promised it would be easy, we were just promised if we learned well, got strong, dedicated, and did our part, we would be rewarded very well for all our efforts. And it would be worth it!

Unfortunately, as we get stronger and more knowledge is added, sometimes we get to thinking we know it all, or enough, and we don't need any more help. That is when evil gets you, becomes stronger, and our struggles continue to test our diligence and desire to remain acceptable to God. So we have to constantly continue learning and becoming better. But we can't stop either, thinking if we do the evil will stop pushing so hard. That doesn't work; it will just over power, and destroy you.

Once we learn to be obedient to the truth, hold true to those laws we have been given, always remembering from whom the laws came, and to whom we owe all that we have, we then are able to act in harmony with His laws. In the end, if we keep at it, we will eventually obtain all we need for our righteous purposes, and receive far more amazing things than we could otherwise ever imagine.

With all these things taken into consideration, we need to then realize that for the most part, all we need to do is ask, and by our words, be able to obtain much of what we ask, as long as it is for those righteous purposes.

Isn't this a wonderful place? Just look around at all the beauty that has been placed here in our temporary home for us to enjoy. If all this is only something temporary that will in time all be done away with – what must our real permanent home be like? That real one we have come here to ultimately inherit. It will surely be beyond our mortal comprehension and earthly understanding, but will absolutely be something I definitely want to obtain, and look forward to.

Come with me, beyond Paradise, to our eternal Heavenly home - in the "country" where our parents live, and they wait for our return.

29-Oct-2010

THE WORD

I used to tell my sweetheart that there was power in words. Over the years, I have come to believe this even more. A word is not just a name, or meaning, or description for something.

And the power of words is not just in how words are put together to say something. Yes, there is power in how they are joined together, and the meaning with which they are said too, but a single word, all by itself, is much more than what we usually think about, and has a power all its own.

This is something most people have never thought about, don't realize, and don't even understand, but I believe is very real. So we need to be very careful how we use words, and what we say.

Realizing this gives even more meaning to what John said in the Scriptures – *"In the beginning was the Word, and the Word was with God, and the Word was God."* In this case, we know the **Word** John was talking about was Jesus Christ, but I also believe, he realized something most people don't, that a single word has a power in itself. (See Matt 12:36-37 - And also remember - by his word Moses parted the Red Sea. 1 Nephi 4:2)

Recently there have been studies done using plants that also tends to illustrate this. As an example, they had two separate groups of plants isolated from each other. They fed and watered both groups identically, but in the presence of one group, they used harsh, degrading words, and with the other, they used soft, tender, loving words. This second group thrived with more luxurious, healthy foliage than the other one, and the only difference was the words that were spoken in their presence.

That is also, why I often tell my children and grand children (and my puppy dog) that I love them. I believe it helps keep them well, and healthy. You can also see what people are like that are always being cussed, cursed, and hollered at. Just imagine how much better those people would be if *just* the language in their presence were changed.

Examples of words that have a great beneficial power are those like – Please, Good, Great, Amen, Honor, and especially *Love*. The power in that one word alone has not even begun to be realized yet by mankind. It is the word used most often by Deity to express their feelings toward all of us, the individuals living on this earth.

And of course, not to be forgotten are the *phrases* like - thank you, I'm proud of you, well done, good job – and especially, *In-the-name-of-Jesus Christ*. That phrase alone strikes fear in Satan and his followers it is so over powering and potent.

There is also the not to be forgotten universal expression that is understood by all people of all languages – the *laugh* – It is very powerful as well. Everyone would be healthier and better off if we could smile more and laugh out loud. If you look at some groups of people with all the troubles they have, you can see they don't laugh much, but how much better they would be if they could find something to smile about. Even in our own groups, things aren't easily found to laugh about any more. That is very sad.

Satan does not like love and laughter, so remember *that*, when you get down and discouraged. Laughter, if you can find it, will brighten your day and bring a good spirit into your life, even if it's just a little smile about the comical predicament you've gotten yourself in, no matter how bad it could be – because, remember, it could always be worse than it is.

It is my desire that we all understand this subtle power we have at our disposal, in our words and attitudes, and use them wisely with great benefit to ourselves, and to all others in the world about us. Now *grin* big!

8-Jul-2006

ONE DAY MANY YEARS AGO

Almost forgotten now (well, sort of,) while living in northern Arizona on the Navajo Indian Reservation, I was bumming around spending a weekend exploring that old and primitive land, when I spotted an old broken and abandoned Hogan. Because I had been told how the Indians constructed their old style Hogan according to their ancient religious beliefs, I was curious if I could see any remains of that structure. It was badly damaged by the weather and nature, and though the dirt covering was mostly collapsed and blown, or washed away by the occasional rain, the original wooden support structure seemed to still be pretty much in place.

First of all, it was facing east as expected, with the door toward the rising sun. The two peeled guardian-angel logs at the entry were visible from where I was, and as I circled the area, I could see most of the other main beams seemed to still be in place as well, which verified what I had been told. The three main support stakes, representing the Father, the Son, and the Holy Ghost were still there supporting the Adam and Eve members; and the roof beams, at the entry, still held most of the small logs, representing the twelve tribes. Most of the other smaller sidewall "sticks" were either gone or still buried in the dirt.

While I was checking it out, looking for anything else of interest, I saw something that looked solid and perhaps metallic peeking out of the ground. It was mostly buried, but of course, it piqued my curiosity. So I kicked at it, not knowing how big it was, or what it was. It moved a bit, indicating it couldn't be too big. So I kicked it some more, and dug at it with my knife blade until I retrieved it out of the dirt, and then discovered it was an old cap and ball revolver. It looked in pretty bad shape, but I wondered if there was anything else of interest around. So I took another, more careful look around, investigating anything that looked out of the ordinary.

Not far from where I found the revolver, I discovered something else. It was almost invisible, blending in with the color of the sand. It turned out to be a book wrapped tightly in oilcloth that was about the same color as the earth it had become buried in.

Actually I didn't know it was a book at first, thinking it might be a box, possibly of tools, or maybe powder, or something for the old gun, until I dug it out and wiped away the dirt and carefully peeled open its covering. Inside was an ancient leather-bound copy of the Holy Bible. Well-worn from use, and the pages slightly smudged with fingerprints of its apparently studious owner, but in amazingly good condition.

As I carefully leafed through the pages, investigating it, another page appeared that was not part of the original book. The paper of this page was also definitely old and somewhat crisp from age as well, but you could tell it was of different origin than the book itself. But having been protected by the book, it was still intact and saved from what would have otherwise been certain destruction. It was folded in half and tucked between the pages of the book.

As I carefully unfolded the sheet to see what it was, it revealed a very beautiful hand written text, which was sharp and clear, but written in such beautiful elegant script it was rather difficult for me at first to decipher what the pen had written. The writing reminded me of signatures I had once seen on an old mid western property deed that had passed from owner to owner, each signature getting more intricate and beautiful the farther back in time you went toward the first owner of the property. This entire page of writing was every bit as carefully executed as were those individual signatures on that old deed from long ago, but the swirls and penmanship of this individual almost made my eyes cross in trying to concentrate on what was recorded there, the writing was so elegantly written.

Not finding anything else, and already having been well rewarded in my search of the day – and excited by my findings, I wrapped the book back up in the cloth as it had been when I found it, picked up the mud and sand encrusted revolver, and headed home to further investigate what I had found.

Since I knew it was going to take some time and study to figure out what was written on that paper, and being a gun guy anyway, I decided to concentrate first on the firearm. To begin with it appeared to be badly rusted and in very serious condition, but since it had already survived, who knows how long, in the harsh high dessert environment, I figured a little more water wasn't going to hurt it that much, so I gave it a good bath.

Surprisingly, as the dirt washed away, I found the outside of the metal was actually in very good shape, and was in pretty good condition, considering, and wasn't hurt that badly. In fact, the outside didn't seem to be rusted any at all. It had apparently been painted with a subtle dark green paint, or at least it was mostly kind of green from something that had protected it from destruction, whether it was paint or whatever it was.

The insides though - the bore, cylinder, and nipples - were quite badly worn away and rusted up, probably from poor maintenance from using corrosive black powder. But overall, considering its probable age the outside of the metal was in surprisingly good condition.

Any wooden grip it may have had was totally gone and there was no hammer or lock work of any kind anymore, that I had found. The smoothly shaped trigger was being held in place with a nail stuck through the frame and bent over on the end to hold it in place, which kept the trigger from becoming lost. The cylinder was rather crudely made, wobbling as it rotated on the pin, but surprisingly tight on the pin except for about 1/16" end play (fore and aft). It had a five round cylinder of approximately 7/16" diameter in each chamber, which would be about .44 caliber, more or less.

The barrel, about 5½" long is flush with the frame without any protruding forcing cone that I could see unless it is internal to the barrel, which has a pentagon shaped bore (I can't tell if there is any twist in the bore because of the rust and crud in there,) but it has an asymmetrical hexagonal shape on the outside.

There is a small brass stud for a front sight and a very tiny niche for a rear sight in the slightly raised top at the rear of the frame. Any loading ram it may have had was missing, as was the lock-work, which must have been a side-hammer since there was no place for a hammer in the frame itself - although there is a hole in the frame for the firing pin to reach through.

I have no idea what it may have originally looked like, but these photographs are what it looked like when I found it (after cleaning it up), and what it still looks like today after these many years.

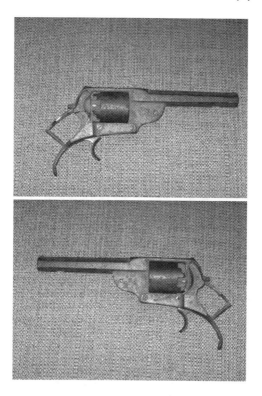

Now after more than half a century, marriage, five children grown and raised, several moves around the country and a sojourn half way around the globe into the Pacific, I still have the revolver. But unfortunately the book and its contents, the drawing of the revolver I made of what I thought it might have looked like in its previous life (before burial,) as well as much of my memory, have apparently been lost to time.

But at least I made a copy of what I believed that special paper to have said, and that has somehow endured along with the revolver. I will copy that paper here as best as I could decipher it for your edification, unfortunately, minus that exquisite handwriting, which was an artistic masterpiece all by itself (and more appreciated by me now than it had been back then.)

I assume it might have been a woman writing it because of the apparent tender insight, though of course I'm not even sure of that, but I will copy it the way I wrote it down, probably with the wrong punctuation, which if there was any, I might not have copied that correctly because of my interpretation and bad English practices. I hope I didn't skip or add anything I shouldn't have, by thinking I would look at it more carefully at a later time, which I never got around too.

She started out by way of greeting, whether to family, friends, or someone else, I don't know, but this is what she wrote:

"To you I wish the blessings of the eternal father in heaven and of his son who came to earth and died for all of us that we might live again after death, as he now does, as was pronounced in this holy book by all the prophets throughout the ages of time. You would do well to search its lines, word by word, as I have done to fully understand what we must do to see them again in their wondrous cities of gold, and feel their amazing love for all mankind, every individual whether living or dead. It is written, there is no deviation in the proper path into that glorious kingdom, but I believe there is a way prepared for me, even though I have never been visited by the angels or prophets, other than by their words here in this holy book. Though I have never been baptized by one having the authority to do this, as he showed we must do, I know I will someday have that opportunity to be washed of my sins, which are too many to numerate, else what shall they do which are baptized for the dead, Paul asked. Then, if I do my part, I could be given the chance to be invited into his household. How wonderful it must have been to live among the prophets, and yet how terrifying to see the destructions caused by the blind people who would not see. There may be prophets now in this barren land that I do not know, and why not? Hasn't there always been, and why not still until the end of time? He is the same yesterday, and today, and forever. He says there are other sheep, and they shall hear my voice. Perhaps I will be among those other sheep and yet meet with him and hear his words for myself. Oh, what a glorious day that would be. I beg you to follow his example that we might all go with him to that magnificent home in the clouds to live with them forever."

I don't know if this was from an Indian (Native American), a missionary, or someone else, but she seemed to have been well educated, and well versed in the scriptures. And which was also quite obvious from the use of the book. I, of course, don't know who she might have been writing to, or if it might have only been a prayer, but the way she ended it, it sounded more like she was writing to someone, or maybe to everyone.

I know that since reading this, I have been more diligent in reading the scriptures, looking for good things and trying to do what God wants me to do, and it has helped me understand things I never had known or been able to understand before – and I am wondering if she was one of those "other sheep" the Bible referred to, and got to hear His words for herself.

I've also wondered; whose revolver this was, and where she-he-or-they; might be now. Hopefully she, or he, is now in that "magnificent home in the clouds", she mentioned, blessed with all the blessings she wished for others.

Unfortunately, the world's history seems to be on a treadmill that just keeps going around and around. We live in a world of wonders, full to overflowing, with great blessings from God, but there are so many, and more and more every day, that are blind to these wonderful things the scriptures say. I wonder how soon the destructions will come again to right the wrongs mankind is bringing down upon our heads. Will we survive the next one?

I guess if we read the scriptures, and do what we are told we must do, they tell us we don't need to fear. At least we as individuals might survive, but the world will never be the way we know it to be now, ever again.

I guess I have to echo the words of the writer above – please, I beg you, for your own sake, and for no one else's, learn what is right and follow his example (the example set by our Lord, Jesus Christ) so you might be able to go with him to that wonderful place in the clouds to live with him forever.

17-Jul-2008

THE ARK

A huge undertaking

The Ark was approximately 450 feet long, 75 feet wide and 45 feet high; plus or minus a few inches I suppose. It was the largest ship ever built until some 3000 years later, again, plus or minus. Imagine 1½-football fields' laying end to end, or better yet, a single building 1½-city-blocks long, ¼-of a block wide, and 4½-stories tall - *that floats*! (Assuming a city block is 300 feet square, and 1 story is about 10 feet high.)

Even by today's standards, it was a huge ship. (*The dimensions of the Ark were given to Noah by God, as shown in Genesis chapter 6, in cubits. A cubit was the measurement from the elbow to the end of the fingers, which varied between 17.5 inches and 21.5 inches. I used 18 inches for my calculations. The ship could have been even bigger than I calculated using that figure, maybe 537 feet long.*) It had 3 levels and each level was divided into rooms. In these rooms there would have had to be room for 2 of every animal, fowl, bird, and creeping thing (or was it 4, **"and there went in two and two, of every sort... male and female"**.) In preparation they would have to accumulate 2 (or was it 4) of each species, except for the **"clean"** beasts, of them there would have to be 7 of each male and female. (Check it out in Genesis, chapter 7.) I'm sure you knew that, right?

On top of all this, there would be 8 people (Noah, his wife, their three sons, and their wives,) and there would have to be food for all the beasts as well as for all of them, enough to last the entire duration – whatever that was going to be. (And I'm sure they didn't know how long they would be there.) And perhaps maybe even a large variety of seeds to repopulate and replenish the earth with vegetation. (Ever wonder what they did for drinking water for that long, sealed up in the Ark?) Do you have your year's supply of food, cash, and water for an impending disaster of some kind? – (As the Prophets warn us we should do?)

It took them a hundred years to build the Ark, but when the time came, they were given only seven days to get all the "beasts," and themselves, on board, before the fountains of the great deep were broken up and the rains came. (And if they figured their days like they did elsewhere in the early scriptures, where a day was morning to night, and another day was from night to morning; that would be only three and a half of our days.) It takes me far longer than that to move my few things into a 2000 square foot house, even at a full 7 of our days.

On the 17th day of the 2nd month (February 17th if you used today's calendar) the rains came and it rained for 40 days and 40 nights (you can bet it really rained too, not like our rains today), until 22½ feet of water covered the mountains. And it pretty well stayed that way for 150 days. (How long can you tread water?) After 5 months (on the 17th day of the 7th month), the Ark ran aground and came to rest on the mountains of Ararat. (And don't forget, this probably wasn't the same mountain we now call Mount Ararat, because it wasn't until about 150 years **after** the flood, during the time of Peleg, that "**the earth was divided**." Before that, the land was all together in one place. So who knows what the earth looked like before it was *divided*, or what all happened when the continents were ripped apart and separated?)

Now, mean while, back at the Ark. After another 2½ months (the first day of the 10th month,) the *tops* of the mountains were seen. Another 40 days later, Noah opened the window and sent out a Raven and a Dove to see if the water was dried up off the earth, but the Dove found "*no-where*" to rest.

7 days later, he tried sending the Dove out again. This time the Dove was able to find an Olive leaf, but yet another 7 days later when he sent the Dove out again, it never came back.

After one whole year and 10 days after it all started, Noah was told they could all leave the Ark. And after building an alter he took some of each of the "*clean*" beasts that were with them and offered burnt offerings to God. (In our day, just as in the past, we are commanded to offer a sacrifice. Only now our sacrifice is work, and of paying tithing which is only a tenth of our monetary increase - which would be so much easier than burnt offering sacrifices would be. But if we do this, it guarantees we will receive even greater, more generous and abundant blessings than we can even imagine.)

Stop and think about all this. Put in terms you might be somewhat familiar with, this was a tremendous undertaking for one man's family, even with the Lord's guidance. (*Nobody else was about to help the crazy old coot build his ship, either.* Right?) But with God's help they did accomplish it, and it was because they believed in Him, and had his guidance.

Yes, God promised he would never destroy all living things again (at least *by a flood)* but he didn't say there wouldn't be serious trouble you would have to live through.

Have you found "***grace in the eyes of the Lord***" like Noah; in this "***corrupt and violent earth***?" Or for that matter, do you have a year's supply of food as the Prophets recommend?

Suppose if there were another flood, an earth quake, or some other great disaster – are you living the kind of life that would allow you into the Ark, or would you get left outside in the rising water, and debris, banging on the closed door? It's better to listen to the Lord and his Prophets, and prepare for whatever is to come – because whatever is going to come, it will come suddenly, with no time left to prepare!

15-Dec-06

MOST RELIGIONS

According to most religions, when you die you either go to Heaven or you go to Hell. They never seem to be able to tell you exactly where that line between the two is though. Since I started out definitely wanting to go to Heaven instead of that other place, I always tried to do my best to stay well up on the right side of that imaginary line.

As you get older, and life's trials begin coming at you so fast, and in so many devious ways, you find out that that line, if there ever was one, fades considerably from view. It is not only more difficult to estimate where it is at; you find that there are all kinds of people and forces pushing you in the wrong direction with the promise that you are still OK, and in acceptable territory – whether you are or not.

Thank goodness for a loving God and His marvelous plan for life and happiness, and finding the one and only true Church of Jesus Christ where all the rules are laid out in a logical, understandable way, with guides (the Holy Ghost, the scriptures, revelations, etc.) and His servants (the Prophets, Apostles, Seventies, Bishops and other leaders) to help us stay on that straight and narrow path that leads directly to that Kingdom where you want to ultimately go – where God the Eternal Father, and His Son Jesus Christ now live in Celestial Glory forever and ever.

Yes, there are other places you can go, if you stray off the path, but there are ways provided for you to get back on the proper road if you do stray, and if you want to – that is if you don't get too mired down in the muck that those places lead you into before you realize you aren't where you need to be. It all boils down to knowing the truth; and what you need to know to obtain the peace you want to get out of life. You must seek for yourself that truth, and the knowledge you need, to keep going in the right direction.

The best place to start that search of course is in the scriptures. This is where the Prophets have written down directions for finding the right path, and how to stay on it.

Then using those scriptures, search out that church established by Jesus Christ himself, and listen to the present day Prophet He has called to lead His Church that covers all the bases needed for us to return to live with our Heavenly Father.

First of all, the Old Testament was, more or less, the temporal law, specifically to tell the people what they needed to know to prepare them for the coming of a Messiah, even Jesus the Christ, who was actually known as God in the Old Testament. He is of course, the one true God of this world. What they didn't seem to understand then, and many still don't today, is that He would be the one to actually come as the Christ himself, to literally set up and establish His Church on the earth while He was here.

Then the New Testament was written specifically for the people who lived during the time while Jesus Christ was on the earth (and thereafter), telling them face to face, what He had been telling the Prophets, from the beginning of time – That, the law of love was much more important than the temporal laws. And that was when He gave them that higher law of love and charity to live by. And along with that, what they needed to do to inherit eternal life (*once he sacrificed his own life for them, why he sacrificed his life for them, how to stay on the correct path he had shown them, and how to get back onto it again if they strayed off the correct path.*)

But this message was also to every one of us that have come since that time as well. Those old temporal laws were not done away with - they had fulfilled their purposes and are still valid today (and for us to still learn from).

But all the things the people were taught and should have done, they didn't do – and then they couldn't anymore because in rejecting him, He took away their blessings of enlightenment.

That was when the authority He had given the Apostles to carry out

His gospel properly was lost, along with all the Apostles He had called to serve in His Church.

But He still didn't stop there. He caused another testament to be written and provided it for us, to set things straight and restore the authority and other important things – again – that were lost during the dark ages since those older testaments had been written.

At the same time, this new testament proved that those originals, and all the things the Prophets had already been saying were still true, and could be believed in - and how necessary every one of those laws, and their proper application are to every one of us, even today.

Included in this "Third Testament," if you want to look at it that way, are all the original doctrines and covenants that had either become corrupt, or were totally lost over time, and from disuse – but are so very important, that they **must** be restored before Jesus Christ can come again the second time.

Remember, the world has already been baptized with water – in Noah's time. We must also be properly baptized with water by emersion, just as Jesus did when he sought out John the Baptist who was baptizing in the Jordan River (because there was sufficient water there for it to be done properly). That is also what we must do. To be found acceptable to God.

Soon the earth will be baptized with fire (when Jesus Christ comes the second time), as we must also do after being baptized with water. This is done for us by "the laying on of hands" to receive enlightenment, and all true things from the one who knows all truth, the Holy Ghost. Something that John the Baptist could not do because he didn't have the proper, higher, authority to do that.

Unfortunately, that authority Jesus Christ had, and that He had given to the Apostles, was soon lost from the world after he was crucified. Because after he was crucified, and the Apostles were all killed, that divine authority that the Son of God had given to the world was no longer available to be passed on, and was missing from the earth, because of mankind's evil and wicked ways. That is why they call it the "Dark Ages" - because there was no "Light" being received from God. (And He withheld his spirit for a long, long time, according to our reckoning of time.)

That was when mankind floundered, seeking the truth and always coming up way too short – until God said it was finally time to be restored again, and then he called a new Prophet. A humble young man with great faith, like the Prophets of old, that hadn't been brain washed by society and the world.

He was ridiculed, made fun of, tormented, tortured, and finally killed because of it. Satan knew what was happening, and he didn't want it to, or what it would bring back to the world. He still continues today in his efforts to try to destroy it in every way he can, and against any who have embraced, taught, shared, or promoted it.

But God's work goes on in spite of Satan's evil efforts, and his attempts at destroying those who want to follow their Heavenly Father and His Son, our Lord and Savior. So that proper Priesthood Authority has been restored again now in these latter days so that all things can be, or soon will be, reestablished and ready for Christ's second coming.

Do you remember Nebuchadnezzar's dream of the great image that Daniel was able to interpret for him; when that rock that was cut out of the mountain without hands, Daniel 2:45 –(*the true Gospel of Jesus Christ*) will roll forth and stand forever, never to be lost again. That part of the plan has already happened, and is rolling forth in our day, even as you read this. Be prepared to meet the Lord when he comes. It will happen suddenly, without warning - other than what we have already been told. Find your way back quickly, if you're not already on that straight and narrow path that leads to eternal life. There will be rejoicing on earth and in Heaven for your obedience, faithfulness, and enduring to the end, if you follow all the rules Jesus has laid out.

18-Apr-2009

MYSTERIES? - NOT!

There are a few things you might have missed, or passed over, perhaps not understanding what was meant, the last time you read the scriptures – You have read the scriptures haven't you? Everyone should read the scriptures you know, they were written specifically for *you* to read so you would know what God wants **you** to know. Too often, we depend on someone else to read them for us and blindly accept **their** interpretation of what is being said.

Unfortunately, that is tragically wrong. The scriptures are specifically written in a way that every time you read them, you find out new things, and you get a better understanding of what is there for you, and what *YOU* need to learn from them. Which also means you should read them over and over many times. Each time (especially in times of turmoil, despair, or distress) you will learn new things that will help you. This is what defines scripture, and distinguishes it from all other kinds of writing.

But for those things you read, that must mean something, but you don't seem to have an explanation handy, it is good to depend on prayer, the Holy Ghost and the Prophets for your daily enlightenment.

For instance: When the disciples asked Jesus about the blind man who was blind from birth *"Jesus answered, neither hath this man sinned, nor his parents…"* (John 9:1-3) How could he have sinned to cause his blindness, if he was blind from birth? The Prophets tell us there is a "pre-existence" where we lived with our Heavenly Father before we came to the earth to be "tested". Apparently the Apostles knew and understood this, they just didn't understand quite how everything worked yet, so they needed help from the Lord – just like each and all of us still do.

In Ezekiel, he is told by the Lord, there should be two sticks (that is scrolls, or books) one for Judah (the Jews) and another for Joseph through Ephraim (Ezekiel 37:15-17). Judah and Joseph are two of the twelve tribes of Israel, and these two books are to be joined together into one in the Lord's hand.

People often think he meant the Old and the New Testaments, but both of these testaments are written essentially by the Jews, and for the Jews, so that can't be true. And in the New Testament, Jesus explained, *"Other sheep I have, which are not of this fold: them also I must bring, and they shall hear my voice; and there shall be one fold, and one shepherd."* (John 10:16)

Even the Jews didn't understand and were divided over this as it says in verse 19. But he further explained, *"other sheep **not of this land**, neither of the land of Jerusalem, neither in any parts of that land round about wither I have been to minister. I go unto them, and they shall hear my voice, and shall be numbered among my sheep, that there may be one fold and one shepherd."* So he was talking about somebody other than the Jews. He was talking about the tribe of Joseph and the book they would write, and it was to come together with the stick of Judah and be one in the Lord's hand.

We are also told: *"In the mouth of two or three witnesses shall every word be established."* (2 Cor. 13:1) This is to bear witness and testify to its truthfulness.

The one I think that is really cool, and helps explain Nebuchadnezzar's dream, and Daniel's interpretation of it to the King (Dan 2:36-45.) – Finally, after describing the figure, in verses 42-44, he tells about the toes of the image. *History* reveals the identity of those 10 kings spoken of, when "the **stone** (the gospel of God's Kingdom) that was cut out of the mountain without hands," will roll forth, not to be left to other people, and then His true gospel would stand forever. Those ten kingdoms, and the years when they became kingdoms are as follows:

1. 496 - Italy
2. 752 - France
3. 803 - England
4. 806 - Belgium

5. 922 - Holland
6. 1138 - Portugal
7. 1139 - Prussia
8. 1159 - Austria
9. 1179 - Spain
10. 1829 - Greece

In the year 1830, an ancient record, hidden in the ground for hundreds of years, with the account of the Lord's visit to the tribe of Joseph was brought forth out of the ground by a new Prophet with the help of an angel of the Lord, and when put together with the stick of Judah, would help reestablish the true Kingdom of God – and this would never be destroyed again.

Since we know God is a man of law and order; it was obvious that not all of the different sects and religions on the earth could be right; there was just too much confusion, disorder and disagreement between them, and what the truth had to be. That is not the way God's Kingdom works. There had to be a correction, and consequently a restoration, of the things that were lost in the "dark ages" after Jesus Christ had first established the gospel when he was living on the earth, and was then lost.

That is one thing the combining of the two "sticks" was to accomplish, literally not only correcting, but consuming those other religions of untruth, which would not "cleave one to another". Actually though, people are so indoctrinated to their false teachings they still do not see their errors or want to correct their ways, determined to prove they are right, no matter how wrong they are. Unfortunately Satan has done a good job of blinding the eyes of man.

In spite of this, the Lord's true gospel would be restored (and has been) and from that point will never be destroyed again as Daniel prophesied. This was necessary so that the world would be ready for Jesus Christ to come again. There is only one way that he approves of, and that is His way, His law, and His gospel – **His** Church of **Jesus Christ**. *"The law of the Lord is perfect."* (Psalms 19:7) *One Lord, one faith, one baptism, one God and Father of all, who is above all, and through all,* (Ephesians 4:5)

That is the problem with man trying to do things and understand what God wants without direction from him. There is **NO one,** except an authorized **Prophet of God** that has been called *by God*, and given the Holy Priesthood through the lineage of Jesus Christ that can speak **for** him and for His Church. Anyone who tries to take that authority upon themselves without His express consent and permission will find they are in serious trouble. *"As we said before, so say I now again, if any man preach any other gospel unto you than that ye have received [from him], let him be accursed."* (Gal 1:9) – This is the word of warning to false ministers who do not bear the Holy Priesthood, and have not been given that authority *from* ***Him***!

(A true disciple, if he bears the priesthood, can show you their line of priesthood authority all the way back to Jesus Christ, the giver of that authority.)

Beyond the administrative law of the gospel however, which is the law to everyone on the earth; personal revelations to you, for your own individual needs, are given only *to you*, only *for* you. That is the reason you need to read the scriptures for yourself, for your own guidance, and not depend on someone else to do that for you, or depend on their interpretation of it.

And remember, you always have the right to pray to him, to ask for his guidance for yourself. *"If any of you lack wisdom, let him ask God, that giveth to all men liberally, and upbraideth not; and it shall be given him.* ***But let him ask in faith, nothing wavering****. For he that wavereth is like a wave of the sea driven with the wind and tossed. For let not that man think that he shall receive anything of the Lord."* (Unless he has that pure faith) (James 1:5-7)

But if you ***do*** exercise that faith, he will surely answer you if you listen carefully, God is not dead, nor does he sleep. He is *the same yesterday, and today, and forever* (Heb 13:8) he does not change. He still, again, has Apostles and Prophets on the earth the same as he did when he lived on the earth. He still cares about you *"this is my work and my glory – to bring to pass the immortality and eternal life of man"* (Moses 1:39) he said, and he wants you to learn what is right for you, yourself, so you can live with him and have great rewards.

The scriptures are full of interesting, enlightening things that will teach you things that those who are too busy, uninterested, or perhaps too lazy or ignorant to find out for themselves. Don't be one of them

-- Your very life (your eternal life that will last for millions of lifetimes) is far too important to take lightly.

What do you suppose this means: *"Else what shall they do which are baptized for the dead, if the dead rise not at all? Why are they then baptized for the dead?"* (1 Cor. 15:29)

Baptism by emersion is one of the **most important** ordinances we must do if we want to become "born again" into the family of God and live with him. But because not everyone had the chance to be properly baptized when they were living on this earth, like your great-great granddad perhaps, they can still be baptized posthumously by a proxy to give them that chance. (They are not condemned to hell just because they lived a couple hundred years ago.) God is a just God, a fair God, a righteous God, a God of love and mercy. Isn't that a wonderful, heartwarming fact to know? Would you have Him be any other way? (Underlines and other formatting added for emphasis.)

29-May-2009

WHAT CAN WE LEARN
FROM THE SCRIPTURES?

What *do* we learn from the scriptures? One thing man learns from the scriptures is, that man learns very little from the scriptures. He just keeps doing the same old things over and over again, and it always ends up in the same horribly tragic way.

If we really read, and take the time to understand what we read, we would be a lot better off, and a whole lot smarter than we think we are.

For instance, I believe the Scriptures give us answers to many questions we have, that we just simply overlook, and wouldn't be so controversial if we took the time to really think about what we are reading. That would help us understand everything that is in there.

So what *can* we learn if we search them carefully?

Well, for instance in 3 Nephi 1:13. Where Nephi was praying about the destruction of the faithful people by the wicked people if the Lord did not come as was prophesied by Samuel the Prophet. It reads, *"The voice of the **Lord** came unto him saying: 'Lift up your head and be of good cheer; for behold, the time is at hand, and on this night shall the sign be given, and on the morrow come I into the world, to show unto the world that I will fulfill all that which I have caused to be spoken by the mouth of my holy prophet.'"* What is that really telling us? Really quite a lot, but you have to think about it a little bit differently than most people do.

That seems to indicate that the spirit does not enter the body, and the fetus does not actually become a soul, until that child is born. We also know that Adam was formed first and then he was given *"the breath of life."* We also know that if our spirit leaves us, we are just a dead body – An empty shell with no life!

So, as I understand it, we can also believe, *in spite of all the emotions involved* (and that can't be taken lightly) if a baby is "still born", that body is not considered a child. But if a baby is born and lives for only a minute or two before dying, a spirit has received that body and is therefore considered a child - even if they actually live united for only those few seconds.

So, it seems, the Lord has already answered the question about when a fetus becomes a **person**, and this is only one of many things we can learn from the scriptures.

But wait! There is more to this supposition – we must also remember, that abortion is an entirely different scenario. Abortion may not destroy a soul, but it surely destroys a body that was being created to house the spirit of one of God's children, and prevents that spirit of having a mortal body in which to dwell – at least for that particular moment in time. We don't know but what the punishment for destroying a suitable body for a spirit, for no good reason, might be just as serious as actually taking the life of a soul once created and joined together (actually killing a person.) Perhaps destroying its chance to be tested and fulfill its proper time in this estate at the moment it should.

This doesn't mean that that spirit might not eventually have that chance, since God's plans are never thwarted, or that the spirit doesn't have a definite influence, or connection to that unborn body even before being born into this world. But, the body that was being formed for that specific spirit was undoubtedly being created especially for the benefit of that particular spirit to fulfill its earthly estate, and at that specific time, with the proper conditions set in place, and they would be quite intimately involved.

As an example; if you were having a house built for you to live in, you would be intimately involved in its floor plan, and how you planned to use it for your purposes. Even though you weren't living in it yet, you might be checking on it to be sure it was what you wanted. You probably picked the contractor and builders you approved of to do the job right, and made sure they put the light switches, fixtures, and faucets where they were supposed to be, and used the right materials to make it strong, sturdy, and able to last a good long time, knowing you would soon take possession.

You might even make a walk through, checking on things, seeing if it was going to fit as the construction proceeded, and be excited to see how things were coming along, even though you hadn't actually taken possession of it yet.

If something happened to that special home, and at the last minute, it was torn down before you were able to occupy it, I can imagine you would be pretty upset about it – to state it very mildly! Could you blame them for getting upset for having their home destroyed, and having to start all over, making all their plans all over again, and finding new builders that would meet all the requirements?

The same could be said for that spirit whose body was prematurely ended. Remember, there might be an extensive network of events in place to furnish that child with all the special opportunities that it needs to fulfill its earthly mission. If those things were upset, how long would it be before all things could again be set in place to accomplish everything necessary for that spirit?

And I must add something else. As a parent and mother preparing a body for a new child to come into your life, be extremely careful of what you put into your own body. Don't just take drugs of any kind, or anything else just to please your own selfishness, to stop a minor hurt or for any other triviality. It may harm, disable, and deform that precious vessel, and not only cause that child misery throughout its life, but you as well having to care for a spirit living in a broken shell.

There are many things about this life we still don't know. So don't mess with them. Concentrate on what you do know to be right. Fulfill your moment in time with the best you can accomplish with what little we know, always looking for the ultimate goal of returning to your Celestial home and the God who gave you this special opportunity of life on this beautiful world created especially for you.

Read the scriptures; take your time to understand the scriptures, and everything they are trying to tell you. They were written for you, and to help you understand everything you need to know.

9-Dec-2007

WHO IS YOUR GOD?

When you are born into this world, you are like a tiny dot on the paper of life. Your memory has been cleaned out so you can learn everything new that you need to know, and write it in your book of life (out of which you will be judged). At that moment, you don't know God anymore, or anyone else. It will take time to learn who He is, and who you are.

As you begin to grow, this tiny dot draws a very fine line in the sands of time. By the time you are one or two years old, you will have learned more in that length of time than will ever happen again in that same span of time at any point anywhere in the rest of your mortal life. And mysteriously that line has begun to widen out a bit.

By the time you are eight years old that line begins to separate into two nearly parallel lines following closely together, but beginning to spread slightly, changing in their appearances and starting to take on separate identities and meanings.

The line on the right has become a sharp brilliant white beam of light that penetrates deep into the distance like a narrow white laser beam, piercing the darkness. The other side, the line on the left, is changing into the opposite, a deep black fuzzy line that also cuts through space. It penetrates the darkness too, but is totally lost very soon in the distance.

Between those two lines is a widening gap that includes a grey area influenced by the sloughing off of the blackness from that black line. However, the brilliant white light is straight and narrow like the sharp edge of a razor blade, undeviating in its power, strength, and purity, seemingly gaining even greater vigor and force the farther it goes, and is totally uninfluenced by the grey that is beginning to fill in the space between the lines and crowding into its side.

The black line has power too, but it is constantly bleeding into that widening gap more and more, filling the gap with a darkening gradient of grey, very, very dark along the side of the black line, and lighter on the side next to the white line, but all the space in that gap is polluted with grey now, right up to the bright white line.

The path of these lines, and the gap between them, is in reality, like the path of life in this world; bright brilliance and light on the right side, blackness, and foreboding darkness on the left, with a gradient of gray filling the void between.

That space between the two lines is a place called "acceptable" by the world. As an eight year old, the space was not well defined or understood. As a teenager, the acceptable void has become even wider and a bit muddy, but to the world, that is acceptable enough.

However, the gradient of the particular path you have chosen to follow might be getting a little darker. It might not even be apparent until you look over at that piercing white line, which seems to be getting farther away.

It might be nice if you could shift your direction more to the right side into the lighter regions of the gap, but the path has become kind of like a rut, hard to get out off, and filling with muck that seems to be hard to pull away from. And the darkness shading your eyes also hinders movement toward the right making a change difficult.

For that reason, it just seems to be easier to sort of drift downhill to the left into the even darker regions than to move up to the lighter side. And perhaps the brilliance of that white line is also shinning in your eyes. And in spite of the good you see in it, you're told and you rationalize it to be pushing you away, and a hindrance.

It's hard to kick off the muck caking around your feet too, so it seems like too much of an effort to struggle against, even though, if you could get up to the brighter side of the gap, your travels through life would be easier and you could see where you are going better.

Unfortunately, time continues on, sweeping you farther into the same direction you have been going. Still, that little bit of light you saw when you made an attempt is encouraging, and that glimpse was enlightening. You feel perhaps the effort might be worth it, and you try again. How bad do you want to be bathed in that light? It is up to you.

Seeing that glimpse of light made you feel better, and you want to be able to share those good feelings with the others around you. To help them also move to the right. But every time you think you have the answers for them, and try to help them correct their path, you find you can't do it for them. They have to want to change their own path, and you can't do that for them. Trying to just tell them what you feel, and they need to be doing, won't help. It is up to them to make up their own minds, and it is their own choice to follow the path they want to follow. Unfortunately they just want you to be on the same path as they are.

And actually, all those who saw you trying to move to the right, away from those things that were acceptable before, don't give a wit for what you are trying to accomplish, or to do now. They couldn't care less about you; they're fine with what they are doing – in fact, now they are condemning you for trying to change your chosen path. They mentally and verbally beat you down for what they previously praised you for doing – trying now to pull you even farther into those darker regions.

It is discouraging and almost too difficult to try, and makes moving to the right even harder. But **almost** is the word you need to concentrate on, because something inside you knows **almost** means it's not impossible, there is **hope** of getting where you want to go, and hope can be stronger when you add faith that you can do it.

Faith is hard to get a hold of, you're not even sure what it is, but if you can grasp a hold of it tight enough, you realize you really can make it. Faith even seems to keep slipping away, but if you keep trying, your grip gets stronger and you hang on longer each time you try, until you are clinging solidly to it, and your grip cannot be pulled away. Yes! Faith is what you need!

If you had only known early on, that being acceptable was just too far away from right, you might have followed a better path – even the right path. Then life wouldn't have been so difficult, and maybe not so loud from all the hollering coming from the dark side. But your struggles have made you stronger, and you hang on. And now, as you pull to the right, slowly maybe at first, you can see farther ahead, toward the light, and that it is good.

Then, with that light, and your maturity, you begin to realize there are two gods at the end of those two lines.

The one at the end of that dark black line is called Lucifer or Satan – and is the dark god of this world – shouting at you with his bull horn, prodding you from his pit of molten tar from which no one can escape from if caught firmly in its grasp.

The other one, the one at the end of that brilliant white line where it explodes into eternity, filling the entire space beyond with dazzling brightness and completely obliterating every bit of darkness, is that kind and gentle God called Father.

He is calmly standing with His hands out stretched encouraging you to come to him. And at his feet is a mountain of blessings that are all yours to have and enjoy, just waiting there for you to receive them.

And if you will, your will is all it takes. You have the power and the ability to choose where you go, and what you will receive. No one can stop you from reaching and achieving whichever place you want to go.

So, what path are you on, where are you headed, who is **your** God? Which line do you wish to follow? Where do you want to end up? The choice is yours, and you have the right, the capacity, the ability, and the capability to follow the line you choose. Choose the Right - and reap the reward of being truly happy forever after!

22- Sept-2009

HOW GOOD ARE YOU

How good do you have to be to go to Heaven? Or put another way, how good do you have to be, to keep from going to Hell? The simple answer to either question is – not very. Not if you don't care what you get, because you've probably already done something to keep you from going to Heaven. And it's already been shown you aren't likely to be bad enough to go to Hell. You see there is more to this simple equation than either - or. It's not as simple as black and white, or yes or no. If you've ever thought about this sort of thing and wondered these things, but didn't have the answers, you didn't understand the whole picture. Let's take a look.

First, you need to understand why you are here. It's not just to fill the space in your shoes. You have a purpose for being. There is a "plan" and a purpose for living.

So, first of all, let's get one thing out of the way.

It is not very likely that you are going to end up in Hell! How do I know that? Because we are not smart enough! Huh? Yes, exactly! The only way that could happen is for you to know absolutely without a doubt that God is real, to have actually seen him, to know that he lives, and is the creator of all things. Not just believe that, but to actually *know* that without a doubt – **and then**, to deny it, as if to say to him face to face that he is not. That is essentially what happened to Lucifer, and why he became the Devil. And for that he will end up in outer darkness, where there is no light, life or anything of any value.

But you probably aren't as bad as it sounds when it comes to Heaven either. You see there was only one person that never did anything wrong, that would keep them from going to Heaven. That was Jesus Christ, who was the only person that was perfect. That means that all the rest of us have done something wrong, even if it's itty-bitty. So that smug person you see looking down their nose at you – they aren't perfect either! So don't let them bad mouth you.

That is what we are all here for, to perfect ourselves, and learn how to make ourselves perfect. That is what we should all be doing, so please - don't bad mouth anyone else either.

What most people don't understand is - there is much more to this thing called life than we have ever imagined. That is why there is that thing called religion, to teach us more of what we don't already understand. And is why there are Prophets, special people who commune with God so they know what it is all about, and can tell us, so we will know too.

If you don't want to know, you don't have to, or to even listen. Most people don't. But then there are those who think they know it all too, or enough, or maybe they just listen to those others who want you to think they know it all.

How can you tell? Do they know the plan that has been laid out for you? Do you, or do they, know the Prophet that has been called and authorized by God to guide, council, and teach his disciples (that is us, His disciples, His students, His followers that desire to learn and know more)?

So what is God's plan? And what does it have to do with us? Very simply put, it is this: We came here, so we could receive a body (just like Jesus did when he was born to Mary), and to learn how bodies are supposed to work to accomplish what we want to do. As we grew and learned more, we learned about good and bad, and that God is everything good, and Lucifer (Satan) is everything bad. We also are here to decide what kind of person we want to be. Do we want to be good enough to go back to live with God in his glorious home in the Heavens? Or are we going to be satisfied to continue living like everybody does here on this earth, with all the same kind of people, for all the rest of eternity with no chance of ever getting anything any better?

How important is all this to you? God had his only begotten son in the flesh *sacrifice* his life to help convince us how important it is. And at the same time, or at least shortly before he gave his life on the cross, he sweat blood from every pore from the anguish he felt, taking upon himself all of our sins so we wouldn't have to suffer like he did (Luke 22:44) But **only** if we accept Him and the sacrifice He made for us. If we don't, then woe unto us, we will probably have to suffer like He did for us, for our own wrongs!

Yes, when we die, we will (eventually) go either to Heaven or Hell. Now we're back to that original question. What so many people don't understand is that there is one Hell, but there are many divisions in Heaven. Since it is very unlikely you will go to Hell, you might want to know more of what Heaven is really all about.

The Prophets tell us there are three major levels in Heaven, called Kingdoms, and there are many other levels in each of those. The lesser Kingdom is called the Telestial Kingdom, and is where those who just don't care (*about anything*) will go (1 Cor. 6:9-11; Gal 5:19-21). (Not good!)

The next greater Kingdom is the Terrestrial Kingdom, and among other things, is where the people believe in Jesus Christ (*but they don't do anything about it*) will go (Matt 7:22). Much like this world we live in here. Which is everybody going different directions, and nobody caring about anybody else, and nobody getting anywhere. (Not much better!)

The highest Kingdom is called the Celestial Kingdom, or "Kingdom of God" and is where the people who do all things that God wants them to do will go (Matt 7:21). It is only here, in this Kingdom, where we will have the chance to be able to again be reunited with our loved ones, and have them at our side forever. If you would never have, or see, your sweetheart again, wouldn't that be like living in Hell? It would to me.

This Kingdom also has three levels, and each one of those requires us to do certain additional things, and is also, why we will need to listen to the Prophets to find out what those things are. (I believe the highest level of this Kingdom is where you have to go before your sweetheart can be with you.) This is one of the most important things to be considered, and something that you most definitely need to check out.

What is it to me that I should care about you, or what you believe? I certainly don't know it all, but I do understand a little bit about the joy that is possible for doing what God wishes that each of us would do. And I want each of you to feel that overwhelming joy as well. That is why I care. It is not for me, it is only for you.

The great thing about it is these things aren't all that difficult to do, as long as we know what those things are and what we need to do. And anyone, and everyone can find what they are, and do them if they really want to. That is God's goal for us, and what he wants us to do.

Another great thing is that he gives us many chances to get things right (**never** *to come back and do them over again*, but to correct our faults while we are still here), and if we work together giving each other help and support, we can all achieve what we want. It is that simple, it is our choice to choose what we want, and where we will go when we leave here.

12-Dec-2008

SO WHAT?

Why is it so important I have **religion** in my life? Why do I need to know about Isaiah, or John, or Noah, or Paul, or Joseph, or anyone of the multitude of others the Scriptures talk about? **So what** difference does it make? Why are they any different than the John, or Tom, or Bob that I know down the block that I wave to when they drive by? **So what** difference does it make to me? Are they really all that important?

Think of those men in the Scriptures as postal delivery people, and each one of them is bringing you a load of mail each day, but none of it is junk mail, it's all packages and envelopes with valid, honest to goodness gifts, checks, or good information in them. I bet you'd be excited to get a few of those, and be anxious to open them up and see what was inside that you were getting each time, wouldn't you? This page you are reading right now doesn't come from anyone matching that status, but I believe the messages they bring contain much more than a winning lottery ticket.

The authors that wrote those 39 books of the Old Testament, the 27 in the old New Testament, the 15 in the newest Testament, the 140 sections of the Doctrine and Covenants, and the 5 in the Pearl of Great Price, were all commissioned by God, who is the Creator of this Universe, the Father of all mankind.

They wrote to tell you their own stories. They have already received their great wealth and untold treasures (whose value is far greater than any lottery ticket) just so you can learn how to get yours for yourself.

Can you imagine how rich someone would have to be if they owned everything in the World? Everything that everyone has ever made or put together, everything that exists in this entire universe? That means everything that all the people in the world now has, and includes every bit of all the gold, diamonds, platinum, palladium, silver and everything else in the entire Universe.

Actually, all of that already belongs to God *right now*, it is *all* his; he owns every bit of it, even what you think you own – it is *all His*! If you have some of it now, it is only being loaned to you for a short time.

But he has promised that all He has you will have also. All of it, every last bit of it, and then some – *and he does not lie*. You see, no matter how rich someone gets, or thinks they are in this world, they will never leave this world with a single solitary penny of it. The only way you'll ever get any of it is directly through Him.

Our Father, who owns everything in this universe, sent his Son to deliver all those special messages to you, which are worth more than all the riches in this world. It wasn't an easy chore for Him. Only a very few people believed Him, and the others ended up killing Him because of it. But because the message He brought couldn't be destroyed when they killed Him, it was left behind, for us to find and use for ourselves. And just as a tiny seed produces a giant tree, so can His message sprout into wealth untold.

His message is kind of, like a treasure hunt or riddle, all in one, because first you have to find the message, decipher it, and then follow it to the letter to earn the right to cash it in. When you realize how valuable it is, though, you will realize it was worth searching for, and following the instructions perfectly.

That won't necessarily be easy, since there will be those who will try very hard to destroy you in your efforts. But those men mentioned above have not only seen the message, they know how to get the treasure, and how valuable it is, and want you to get it for yourself – so listen to them.

And the important part of this message is, that when you get ready to cash it in, you will find it is worth even more than you could have ever imagined. It is everything like God has – *everything*, and you can receive every bit of it, for yourself also. All you have to do is follow the directions.

So, you see the value of this simple message is also worth untold wealth. It is given free to all for finding, and is more valuable than it appears at first glance, so what this all boils down to is, **that's what**!

2-July-2009

CHOICE

If you had your choice, what would it be? Actually, you already have your choice. God, your Heavenly Father, has already given you the right to make a choice, and you chose what you wanted for yourself. It's called "free agency." You have that free agency to choose for yourself everyday what you want, and what you want to do.

You see in the "pre-existence" (that's where we all were before we came here) we were given a choice to choose what you wanted to do, and get out of life. (That life is here, in this world, this existence where we are now – but it is also much more than that, because what happens here will determine the kind of life we will have after we leave here – *that* life will last for all of eternity).

It was a simple choice there, between those two things. - Come here and be tried and tested to see if we wanted never ending glory, or just be satisfied with what somebody threw at us.

Well, it seems simple enough now. But it was probably really scary at the time, just like some of the choices we have to make here, probably because we really didn't know that much about it then yet. Or if we would be able to handle this life and do what was expected of us. But looking back, I know some of us made the right choice then – because now we're here, living this life, that can earn us so many absolutely wonderful rewards in the life yet to come.

Today we still have some very important choices to make, and those are scary too. They seem so complicated sometimes. Unfortunately, it seems there is no one here that can teach us properly about all the things we need to know. Probably, because they don't know what's right themselves. And without being taught properly, how can we expect to know what we are supposed to do?

Actually though, there are people and things here to learn correct principles from, but sometimes it seems like we have to learn by trial and error, hoping we'll make the right choices or be able to correct any errors we make later. That can be the wrong way to go, because once something is done the wrong way, it is much, much harder to undo it and make it right.

Maybe that's when we need to just stop and think, and use our brains. Stop before we go too far in the wrong direction. And think about the consequences of doing it wrong. That may be the best way to go anyway, because then you have it properly set in your mind about what the right choice is - and next time you will know immediately.

And don't forget, we also have the Prophets and the scriptures to tell us what is right and wrong. We need to study them diligently so when something pops up in front of us, we will know which way to turn.

Unfortunately, Satan doesn't want you to stop and think about it. He doesn't want you to have any choices. He wants you to jump at it and do something stupid before you take the time to use your brain. And he sure doesn't want you to be someone that is so crazy in the head that you get *religious* or something terrible like that - what could be worse than that?

To him, of course, there isn't anything worse than that, and by that same token, there is no one worse than Satan.

Then there are those who have been influenced by him that think they know it all, and try to convince you to do things you shouldn't because, I guess, they don't want to be the only ones stuck in their puddle of muck. And they sure don't want anybody to think they're *religious* or something either!

So what were those two original choices? If you have children, you know you want your children to make the right choices, because you know if they choose wrong, they will have to pay the consequences. If you still don't have children, but have loving parents, you know they want you to make right choices too, and don't want you to have to pay for any bad consequences. They want you to have rewards instead (sometimes called blessings) for doing things right. And that's what God wants too.

That simply was what the two choices were, to always have a choice, even if there was a possibility of doing things wrong that we might have to pay for; or never having a choice of our own and just blindly doing what someone else said we had to do. (There is already too much of that in this world, and I can't think of many things worse.)

In that pre-existence, God had many children and wanted them (us) to grow up and become good people, just like Himself, and probably wanted our opinion about what we thought should be done to help us do that.

Jehovah, who is one of our brothers, and also a Son of God, wanted you and me to have our own choice to do what we wanted to do, and thereby get all the rewards we could possibly earn by doing good things, and we would only have to pay for the things we did that were wrong.

But Lucifer, another brother who was also there, didn't want anyone to have a choice. He wanted to make everybody do everything his way, and would make sure they did, taking away our free agency. And because he would do that, he wanted all the rewards just for himself.

God, being fair in all things, didn't agree, but he let us decide what we wanted to do. Did all the rest of us want to choose the way of Jehovah, or did we want to do things Lucifer's way? We had our own choice.

Just like all the people here, everyone had their own idea about how everything should be done. Some of us were on each side of the question, some were in the middle that were afraid to go either way, and everybody else was everywhere in between.

They say roughly about a third of them leaned toward Lucifer's way, I don't know how many were sitting on the fence in the middle, maybe another third, but the rest of us were inclined to follow Jehovah's way. And here we are, still having the choice of choosing what we want to do, and earning rewards for the good choices we make - *when they are good choices.*

Not only that, because we followed Jehovah's way, He said He would pay for all our mistakes for us, if we accept Him as our "Savior", and follow the example He sets.

That sacrifice He performed for us is what is called the "atonement."

Imagine if you can, the love it would take for just one person to pay for *everybody else's* debts. How could anyone of us refuse an offer like that? Unfortunately, a lot of them did, apparently not having enough guts and strength of their own to resist a "free lunch."

Because Jehovah was willing to do such a marvelous thing, He became known as the Messiah, and given the task of laying out the Church of God on the earth. Later when He came to live on the earth for Himself, He became the Christ, and was given the name of Jesus.

To then pay for all the wrongs from everyone who committed their life to follow Him and accept Him as their Savior, He had to bear everyone's punishment all by Himself. He did that in the Garden of Gethsemane where the punishment was so terrible and severe He actually bled from every pore, actually sweating blood, so we wouldn't have to.

And as if that wasn't enough to do for us, He then allowed Himself to be crucified on the cross (one of the most inhumane methods of torture ever conceived by man to cause a person's death) to show that after we die, everyone of us that have ever lived, or will ever live on the earth (no matter how bad we are) will have our spirit restored to a new body.

Those who have done what they are supposed to, will not only receive that new body, they will also be able to return to live in a Heavenly home (according to our faithfulness) where we will receive untold treasures that **we, *and He*,** has earned ***for us***. And ever since then, the church of God that He had established on earth has been called The Church of Jesus Christ. The only one that is valid to God and worthy to bear His sacred name.

Because Lucifer, who also received other names and is now known as Satan, or the Devil, was so selfish, mean hearted, and even actually rebelled against God and his ways; he and all those who followed his bad example, will never come to the earth to receive a body, and ended up with no rewards at all – not even the right to earn any.

Oh, they are here too, but only in spirit, tormenting the rest of us for having followed God's ways and accepting Jehovah's much better plan.

When they were cast out of heaven for their disobedience, they were so angry they vowed to destroy as many of us as they could, *hoping* we would never earn any rewards either.

God wouldn't just let them force us to do anything bad, but he has allowed them to test and tempt us to see if we would continue to choose what was right or wanted to go the other way. – And from that day forward, they have tried to deceive everybody they could by telling us lies, being deceitful, and making things that are bad, look really, really good, so we wouldn't know and maybe pick the bad things instead. That is why we need to stop and carefully think about what we are doing, and always be sure to choose the right way.

Since there is a right and wrong way of doing everything we do, and though our choices can now be terribly difficult and confusing sometimes if we don't pay attention, we still have the right to choose for ourselves and make our own choices in everything we do. God has also given us Prophets and the scriptures to guide us, if we listen to what they say, and we will be rewarded greatly for making the right choices. I hope your choice is like mine, to receive as many of God's rewards as possible.

9-Nov-2008

PRINCIPLES AND ORDINANCES
OF HIS CHURCH

The first principle of the Gospel of Jesus Christ that we need to understand is to have faith in Jesus Christ. That is to realize that He is the literal Son of God. And understand that He is the physical creator of this universe and this earth. But most importantly, that through Him, and only through Him, can we be saved from our wrongs, the fall of Adam, and be able to return to our Heavenly Father's Kingdom. *"Jesus saith unto him* [Thomas], *I am the way, the truth, and the life: no man cometh unto the Father, but by me."* (John 14:6)

This testimony of, and belief, or faith in Jesus Christ can be achieved through several ways, such as teachings from, and belief gained from someone who already has faith in Him, but mainly from reading the scriptures. Or even inspiration from the Holy Ghost. However, having "Faith in Jesus Christ." is a personal thing, and it is the first of the essential steps.

Once you have faith in Him and desire to follow His example, you recognize that you aren't perfect, that you, as everyone else, have done things that aren't totally correct. *"For all have sinned, and come short of the glory of God;"* (Rom 3:23), so then you realize you need to ask Father in Heaven for forgiveness for doing those wrong things, and of course, promising you will not do them again - and then never doing them again. This is called "Repentance" and that is the second step.

The third step is "Baptism by immersion" (to be laid down in, and be brought back up out of the water, as if being *spiritually* buried and resurrected and/or being born again into a new life) for the remission (removal) of your sins, and take upon yourself the name of the Lord. And then, after accepting Him and being baptized, be numbered among His disciples, and follow Him and His teachings. *"John did baptize in the wilderness, and preach the baptism of repentance for the remission of sins."* (Mark 1:4) *"Therefore we are buried with him by baptism into death: that like as Christ was raised up from the dead by the glory of the Father, even so we also should walk in newness of life. For if we have been planted together in the likeness of his death, we shall be also in the likeness of his resurrection:"* (Rom 6:4-5) This is often spoken of as being "born again" as Jesus told Nicodemus that he had to do, it wasn't just a verbal commitment, but the physical action of baptism, and then following His example.

But John the Baptist said baptism by water was not even enough, we also had to be baptized of the Spirit. *"I [John] indeed baptize you with water unto repentance: but he that cometh after me is mightier than I, whose shoes I am not worthy to bear: he shall baptize you with the Holy Ghost, and with fire:"* (Matt 3:11) And Jesus confirmed it. *"Jesus answered* [Nicodemus] *Verily, verily, I say unto thee, Except a man be born of water* **and** *of the Spirit, he cannot enter into the kingdom of God."* (John 3:5) So, this fourth step is ***the laying on of hands***, by one with that authority from God, to receive "the gift of the Holy Ghost." This is the baptism of the Spirit where we learn we are actually, literally, spirit children of our Father in Heaven; that we are all brothers and sisters of a wonderful God, who loves and cares about us.

And shortly thereafter, hopefully, we receive the "fire" that John speaks of. This is the cleansing and simple realization of all these things, and fills us with the Holy Ghost, which is the spirit of truth, and the desire and drive to become better in every way. To continually strive toward perfection, not only spiritually, but by the company we keep, our actions, and the things we do (our works (see Rev 20:12)), so that through these things, and by the grace of God, we will actually be able to dwell with Him in His Kingdom when we are through with this mortal life. The Holy Ghost then stays with us as our constant companion, if we continue to be good and do what is right. If not, He will leave us to our own devices.

We have to realize though, and remember, that no matter what we do, how good our "works" are (*which are extremely important*), and no matter how perfect we become, it doesn't entitle us to live with God. It is only then, after we have proven ourselves worthy, and done all that *we* are supposed to do, and can do, that it is still only *by the grace of God* that we can be admitted into His Kingdom. "*Wherefore, my beloved brethren, reconcile yourselves to the will of God, and not to the will of the devil and the flesh; and remember,* **after ye are reconciled unto God,** *that* **it is only in and through the grace of God that ye are saved.**" (2 Nephi 10:24) The final judgment of who we are and have become, is **His, and His alone.** You better be on His side!

Titus Chapter 3:1-9 says:

1. *PUT them in mind to be subject to principalities and powers, to obey magistrates* [obey the laws of the land], *to be ready to* [do] *every good work,*

2. *To speak evil of no man, to be no brawlers, but gentle, shewing all meekness unto all men.*

3. *For we ourselves also were sometimes foolish, disobedient, deceived, serving divers lusts and pleasures, living in malice and envy, hateful, and hating one another* [committing sins].

4. *But after that the kindness and love of God our Saviour toward man appeared,*

5. ***Not by works of righteousness which we have done,*** *but* ***according to his mercy*** *he saved us, by the washing of regeneration* [Baptism], *and renewing of the Holy Ghost* [Laying on of Hands];

6. *Which he shed on us abundantly through Jesus Christ our Saviour* [the atonement];

7. *That being justified* ***by his grace,*** *we should be made heirs according to the hope of eternal life.* [To live with God, in His Kingdom.]

8. *This is a faithful saying, and these things I will that thou affirm constantly, that they which have believed in God might* ***be careful to maintain good works.*** *These things are* ***good*** *and* ***profitable*** *unto men.*

9. *But avoid foolish questions, and genealogies* [such as perhaps claiming you were born of someone famous and therefore you don't need to do these things], *and contentions, and strivings about the law* (murmuring and complaining about God's laws and ***the things he says you must do***); *for* ***they are unprofitable and vain.***

[All underlines, explanations and emphasis, of course, are added.]

In other words, after we have obeyed these principles (rules) and ordinances (our works) we are expected to continue in that new direction. But, because we are humans, and are being tempted by Satan continually, who wants us to stray from Christ at all cost, we go to Church regularly and each week are given the opportunity to partake of the Sacrament, the taking of bread and wine (or water, now that our water is safe to drink and we don't have to depend on alcoholic wine), which was instituted by Jesus Christ himself, which is the renewal of those vows and promises we made at baptism to help us stay on that straight and narrow path. *"And as they were eating, Jesus took bread, and brake it, and blessed it, and gave to his disciples, and said, Take, eat; this is **in remembrance of my body which I give a ransom for you.*** [and the wine or water] *In the same manner he took the cup. This is **in remembrance of my blood** of the new testament, which is shed for as many as shall believe on my name, for the remission of their sins. And I give unto you a commandment, that ye shall observe to do the things which ye have seen me do, and bear record of me **even unto the end**.* (Matt 26:26; 1 Cor. 11:24-25; 3 Ne 18:11) and we need to do it often.

The "new testament" He speaks of in these quotes means this taking of the "Sacrament" that replaces the "sacrifice" of the first born of the flock, or fruit of the field, which they had been doing from the beginning of time, which was in similitude of the sacrifice which Jesus Christ himself, being the first born of God without spot or blemish, would do for us.

Along with partaking of the Sacrament at this church meeting we are taught, educated and encouraged by others who are also striving along the straight and narrow path, by giving talks on various subjects as requested by the Bishop, or just bearing their testimonies (stating their beliefs) in the truthfulness of the Gospel, and these things. The Bishops (who aren't perfect either, and are striving along with all of us) are all unpaid volunteers, as are others in leadership positions in the Church, called to their leadership position under the direction of the Lord by those in authority above them, and by the "laying on of hands" (to help them in their perfection as well.) No one is paid to fill these positions, but work at other jobs during the week, the same as everyone else in the world should be doing. And just like the members in the ancient church did.

This might be a good time to mention responsibility. We are each responsible for our own selves, and our families. We should do everything we can to make sure we all are safe and cared for, but we are truly our brothers keeper as well, in that, if someone who is faithful, but having difficulties, not of their own doing (not someone just looking for a hand-out,) we try to step in and help them out temporarily if we can without ever worrying about payback. We are all brothers and sisters in the family of God, and we should each remember that, and act like it. Not act as the world does in a dog eat dog environment.

This is a very brief and very simple explanation of things that all people need to know about the gospel of Jesus Christ, there are several (many) other things required of us to reach the place in God's Kingdom we strive for, but the unique and marvelous thing about the Church of Jesus Christ is that there is no limit or end to the things we can learn pertaining to eternity and eternal life. So these are just **some** of the principles and ordinances we must do to enter back into His Kingdom to live with Him. Learn all you can, while you can, before the night comes.

18-Feb-2008

ACCORDING TO THE LAW

To fully understand what I wish to present in this paper, there are certain important things that need to be established first. So please open your mind to concepts that might be foreign to our mortality - and don't allow prejudices put there by other's flawed beliefs cloud your mind. To begin with, there are at least two truths that you need to understand.

The first is one that many people have not allowed themselves to fully accept, because they can't quite understand, or define it in human terms. That is, that there **really *is*** a God of our universe. And even though He is also a man much like anyone of us, He is a perfect man, a Supreme Being over all things, whose knowledge, wisdom, and abilities, are so far advanced and immense in scope that our tiny minds cannot even begin to grasp or understand them. It is this Supreme Being that created everything we know, and from whom all ***good*** things come.

The second truth may be as difficult, or maybe even harder, to comprehend than the first. It is that there are opposing forces constantly working to tear down, disrupt, and actually destroy all good things, and attempting to cause an eventual collapse of all that is good. This is plain simple fact that defines the struggles of the mortal world that we all face when we are born on this earth.

This resistance, to the good, becomes stronger every day in opposition to the increase of good that we are allowed to receive from our creator, and is actually provided to us, so we can learn right from wrong. We must choose for ourselves which direction we wish to travel, and not only, for in this world, but in the eternities that follow. This is all according to God's law.

To go on from here, we must eventually die, and that is part of life. However, the choices we make here will determine what will come in the next step of life, which follows this one.

I must stop here to make a very important point. There will **never** be a second chance, to come back here, to do this earthly life over again. Anyone who believes in "reincarnation" in this life has been sorely misled into believing if they make a mistake, they can just keep coming back and trying it over and over until they get it right.

That is a falsehood, thrown at the world by the opposition to truth. The fact is, you **won't ever** have a chance to do things over, but you **can** choose to correct errors you've already made, right here, right now – and **only** now. And that will determine where you go from here. That is why this treatise, and this life, is so important, and why you must make the **most** of the very limited time you have here on this earth.

Evil doesn't want you to succeed. He wants you to fail, and when he gets you to fail, he doesn't want you to know you can correct things here. To die thinking you are going to get to come back and try again is another one of his snares. If you do wrong, and then die, he believes he's got you for good, so he uses fancy ideas like reincarnation to deceive and destroy you.

Don't fall for his deceit and lies. Now is the time for you to learn all you can, to correct any flaws in yourself that you can possibly discover. No one has ever said that you will get another chance, so don't plan on it.

That doesn't mean in this life. For as long as you are alive and breathing in this life, God will help you do every good thing you desire, here and now. He wants you to succeed.

Now, if you keep an open mind to the concepts presented here, hopefully, you will come to understand, that the human body in which you find yourself, is as complex as the Universe in which we live. Yet, at the same time, how simple it is once you realize for what purpose it was constructed. Likewise, how magnificent the wisdom and intelligence is of the Supreme Being who created all things. And how understanding this, you can have an even better life then you thought possible, that will carry you throughout this mortality and properly prepare you for the next step in your eternal life.

Just as new bits and pieces are still being found inside of the tiny atom, miracles are also being found in the human brain and body which no one totally understands. For instance, every part of the body is intimately connected to every other part of the body in a complex network of not only muscles, veins, and nerves, but of energy paths, many of which are not easily detectable – but are all constructed according to God's laws.

The science of iridology is only one such illustration of the interconnection of body functions, wherein the iris of the two eyes are maps of the condition of all the parts of the body. This is one of few methodologies where this diagnostic indication can actually be seen so clearly, and then read by one trained in this method.

But just as this interconnection between parts of the body are illustrated in iridology, and can be used to determine where a problem may exist, these types of interconnections can also be found, and used, by some of the other sciences as well. For instance in things like Chiropractic, Reflexology, and Acupuncture.

Sometimes the change that is needed to correct a condition can be influenced by something so infinitesimally small that modern science can neither detect it, nor describe what it is, or how it could possibly work. Homeopathy is one such science that can actually **cure** a condition, restoring health without causing side effects or complications – because there are no side effects caused from them. They just use the forces from corresponding elements without actually adding anything except those tiny imperceptible unidentified energies.

And Feng Shui, an ancient art of using minuscule energies from all the objects around you to control your environment, is another. Just because something can't be seen, or explained by the eyes and understanding of mortal man, doesn't mean it is not true.

Even, or should I say especially, faith in God has caused great miracles to come about. This is one of the greatest gifts of healing there is, especially when administered through the Holy Priesthood of God. (More on energies in a bit.)

To back up a moment, and understand something else about the basics, is that each of us is constructed from two parts. I am **not** talking about the mother and father that were required to produce a living breathing human being unique to the animal world, even though you do contain attributes of each of these individuals.

At the time of the creation and construction of a human child, specific keys were prescribed by that Supreme Being (I will hereafter call God), to give that child a physical body with either dominant male or female characteristics. (And it will be a human body, not an animal of another kind, even though it will be made out of all the same elements.) However, that *body* is only a physical body with bones, flesh, hair, and organs that are necessary to carry out a physical mortal life. In essence, you could even call it a "growth" attached to the mother, much like a mole, or wart, or tumor (before it is born) - of course with much more significant features, and of course, it also has great emotional significance too, unlike those other items mentioned. Still, there is no actual "*life*" in that body, other than that of the mother to which it is connected.

At the moment of the actual birth of that body, however, is when God gives that body a spirit. That other most important part, that makes that body an individual; with passions, personality, thoughts, and ideas of its own. Not fully developed as to human mortality yet, of course, but still with those significant individual traits that make it a unique individual with characteristics borrowed from both the father and the mother, but uniquely and significantly different than either one of them. These are the two parts I am speaking of; the *body*, and the *spirit*. (See also the paper called "What can we learn from the Scriptures") The ancients might call these two parts the yin and yang, the yin being the spirit and female traits; and the yang being the physical and male traits, which are both needed and designed to keep all things in balance and make it a viable human being.

This child will now need to be further developed physically and emotionally, of course. But now, still has its God given freedom of choice, to choose pretty much, what it will do in this mortal life. – (And *please,* don't forget, *training* properly is of the upmost importance to this new child if he or she is going to become the great individual they have come here to be – don't deny them that right now that they are here.)

The spirit part of this equation is the original part that was created of "intelligence" by God, forming an individual spirit that inherently has its own unique traits and talents. It is known that the physical body that was created for it would look just like that spirit would, if we could see it, but the spirit is of a finer material that usually cannot be seen by mortals. We, as mortals, don't really know what "intelligence" is either (as can be proven by reading the newspaper, or watching TV), or how that was all done, but we do know that God knows, and we know it to be true because – we have now been created, the two parts united, and here we are!

Evidence of these facts – there being two parts of each individual – are obvious when you stop to think what happens when the spirit is removed from the body. If, and when, that happens, the body is left alone, without life – dead! The body cannot continue to live without a spirit present, and likewise if the body is severely damaged, or deteriorates to the point it cannot contain the spirit, the spirit is forced to leave, bringing death to the body. (Likewise, if the body does not receive a spirit at the time of birth, the body will be "still born". For the purpose of this paper, we'll assume the spirit has been received by the body, and has given life to the body.)

In this mortal, temporary world our bodies cannot live forever, because being a temporary existence, all mortal things have an end, will deteriorate, and return to the earth and elements from which mortality comes. However, the **spirit**, being made of intelligence and spiritual matter, is *not* mortal, and therefore has no end. Once created, the spirit shall exist forever, even after it has been removed from the body into which it might have been placed.

That is another reason for proper training. You aren't just training them for this life, but forever – *it is that important*! Do it right! – To the very best of your ability.

Knowledge of all these things is important to understand, and will contribute to this child growing into a mortal human being with the potential of fulfilling this life in a manner that also helps fulfill its purpose of creation. For some, this life might only be for seconds, for others, it might be for well over a hundred years.

Understanding that there are two different parts – separate – but combined, and the significance and purpose of these parts, will help you understand the importance of maintaining health and strength in the body, to ensure there will be a safe haven for the spirit to dwell in for as long as possible, while on this earth. If there is something that upsets that balance, and would cause a disruption, then there would be a lack of ease, which is called dis ease, or disease. The purpose of this treatise is to help you understand the balance needed to prolong the life of this mortal body properly for as long as it is allowed to live on this earth, and is why we need to learn how to strengthen and nurture the body in which our spirit resides.

Mankind's contrived "Drugs", which have become rampant in our society, which are prescribed to cure every imaginable symptom; or which find their way into our systems sneakily through food, air, or water; or those which are introduced stupidly by an individual to alter the state of well being into some fantasy existence, are some of the greatest causes of dis-ease. (Also see the paper called "What Can We Learn from the Scriptures" for another very important note on this.)

These things are man's attempt to play god, trying to put together their own form of life. That will never happen, and their attempts instead usually create or cause the breakdown and disconnection of the bodies systems which results in what we call diseases.

Unfortunately, most "medical" drugs are only used to treat *symptoms*, the outward manifestation of the problem, and **do not** "*cure*" the faults that *cause* a disease. It is understood that some drugs can counteract the *symptoms* well enough that they *appear* to resolve a problem, but usually they instead cause many other, seemingly unrelated, difficulties, and side effects. And without getting to the root of the problem will instead cause a snowball of problems that are not only difficult to isolate and eliminate, but the problem just continues to grow and spread, *underground,* manifesting itself in other ways. This is why natural means and methods are always far better than trying to *cover up* a problem with drugs.

For the most part, God has given us all the things we need to help ourselves, such as the fruit of the trees, and the herbs and grains of the field (which I will only mention here.)

And as mentioned, one of the most subtle forms of healing is done through the unseen energies God bathes the world in. His *love* is perhaps the greatest and strongest of all these energies, and he gives it to us freely, and lavishly.

It is so strong, and has so many facets we don't understand even a little part of it, but among other things, it is what keeps the moon in orbit around the earth, and the earth and other planets in orbit around the Sun. (It isn't just gravity and centrifugal forces, which are other laws in God's creation.)

It is also the force that keeps the spirit and the body connected together, in harmony, and in balance, with each other, and with our surroundings, if we will only utilize this information. (By the way, those planets and other heavenly bodies in our solar system also have an effect and influence on each of us that live on this earth. These are tiny, positive, necessary influences for our good, and that is why they are there, they are all according to God's law, and a part of His great overall plan.)

The Sun of course, is also a constant source of nutrition and energy that comes from God over millions of miles of space to all things, continually flowing to the earth, and is needed for both the body and the spirit to live and exist. The Sun never goes out, but the earth rotates so each side gets its share without burning up from the Sun's intense power, and giving an equal period of rest in between.

Next perhaps is another of the essential energies that are absolutely required for human life. It is the oxygen we breathe. This element clings to the earth, supplying a needed nutrient to all living things. Without oxygen, we would die very quickly. But usually we aren't taught how to use it properly for our health and well being, and how it is needed in every part of our body to keep the balance between the body and spirit.

Oxygen is one of the elements that are sort of a combination of spirit and matter. (Actually, spirits are matter too, but of such fine material that mortal eyes can't usually see it.) Oxygen meets this definition very well, being invisible to us, but having weight and substance, and is almost like food for us, nourishing both the body and spirit, and must be carried by the blood to every part of the body. Without it, human life as we know it on this earth would not be possible.

If we don't have enough oxygen in every part of the body it will cause a dis-ease in that part, so it is very important to be sure each part receives its needed amount.

Water may be the next in importance for us in this mortal life.

Water is not only made up of oxygen, it is combined with another of the ethereal (spiritual) elements, called Hydrogen.

Together these two spirit-like, unseen elements, known by themselves as gases, combine together and then appear as something we can now see and also use for our benefit. And here again, water is so important that without it, mortal life would quickly end.

Not the last of the needs we have to sustain mortal life, but an important one, is food of all varieties. Mortality is not something eternal, and as such, it was created to be temporary. In a temporary world, all things grow, reach a peak, then deteriorate or fail, and eventually die. Some sooner than others, but all things have their earthly cycle. So to prolong life for us, for the period needed to fulfill our existence on earth, we need to replenish the parts of us that deteriorate, with new material that is constantly being created for this purpose.

So God keeps sending life to plants, which themselves live and die for the express purpose of furnishing food for us to use to replenish and renew our own lives. Isn't it amazing how from a tiny seed, a magnificent tree might grow with dozens of fruits with their own multitude of seeds that can each do the same thing over and over again. This is all done according to God's Laws. It is not an accident of "nature."

We really don't understand, nor do we really need to know, how it all works, other than to know that God *is*; that He is watching over his children, and taking care of His creation. That He knows all things, has given us all things, and has set up this world for us to use for our own purposes. Our God, the Supreme Being, has created this beautiful world for us, and for our use; "*To bring to pass the immortality and eternal life of man*" Moses 1:39.

(Please understand - in the scriptures, man is a generic term meaning mankind. Women are never excluded or ignored. They are every bit as important as men. Here again, Satan has done his best to cause trouble, and "mankind" has grabbed it and run with it, making a big deal out of nothing!)

There are many things we need to do to fulfill all the things we are on this earth to accomplish, not only for ourselves, but also for our God. That would be a huge treatise all its own, and outside the scope of this one, so I will go on.

Eventually we wear out, and life can no longer continue, but we need to try to keep going until we have done everything we came here to do. To do that we need to take all things into consideration, to learn how to utilize what we have been given, and to maintain and keep a healthy and viable body to house our spirits in for as long as necessary.

It is a temporary world for our temporary bodies to temporarily house our spirits to gain knowledge and wisdom (which lasts forever) from that Supreme-One who has already gained all these things for himself.

To maintain this temporary state for as long as necessary, we need to utilize the energies God provides for us. Healthy, natural foods to repair and replenish our bodies, water to supply those nutrients, oxygen to convert the fuel into the building blocks, and those other unseen energies to help nurture, refine, and perfect us, if we can.

There are multitudes of different natural sciences that deal with these things. Some of the ones I have studied include; Massage, Interferential Electrotherapy, Ultrasound, Chiropractic, Light, Rolfing, Numerology, Reiki, Iridology, Phrenology, Graphology, (applied) Kinesiology, Reflexology, Homeopathy, Acupuncture, Qigong, Hypnosis, Acupressure, Tai Chi, Feng Shui, crystals, and of course plain Vitamins and Herbs. Which really, are not all that plain, simple, or insignificant (and you might notice I didn't directly mention the "medical profession which I believe is often way too contrary to the promotion of *real health* and a *good life*.")

Thought waves alone, can be used to beneficially influence the health of a person. Like radio waves that can't even be seen, a person can learn how to send out healing energy to heal a body that is in disease – or can use it in a bad way to tear it down.

Several of those listed above are ancient arts that use subtle exercises, methodical manipulations, and various other natural techniques, mainly to nourish the body and spirit with oxygen, and to heal and promote freely flowing energies to all parts of the body for our health and well being. I have examined and investigated many of these for my own reasons and purposes (though mostly to help my Sweetheart get through this sometimes miserable life.)

There are probably even some I've forgotten, and of course, the ones I've touched on are only a few of the probably hundreds that are out there.

The most important and significant fact is that, for the most part, they use principles derived from following God's laws, rather than mankind's artificial contrivances. I believe we would all be better off if we could concentrate on, be obedient to, and live according to God's Laws - all of them. Then we will be blessed far beyond measure.

20-Feb-2010

ONE OF GOD'S LAWS

God's laws are often really very simple. So simple our mortal minds have a hard time grasping them, and they seem contradictory in the language of man (influenced by the Devil himself, who is also known as Lucifer, Satan, and a few other nasty names.) Earthly logic, which often seems to be so very reasonable and predictable at times *can't* be depended on to understand Heavenly truths.

Take for instance what Malachi says in the 3rd chapter in the last book of the Old Testament of the Bible. (By the way, you do know, don't you, that the books of the Bible are not in chronological order? The book of Malachi was written long before some of the other books in the Old Testament. Just like Revelation, the last book placed in the New Testament, was not the last book written before the apostasy and fall of mankind into the Dark Ages. It was actually written long before most of the other books in the New Testament. - Now back to what Malachi told us.)

8. *Will a man rob God? Yet ye have robbed me. But ye say, Wherein have we robbed thee? In tithes and offerings.*
9. *Ye are cursed with a curse: for ye have robbed me, even this whole nation.*
10. *Bring ye all the tithes into the storehouse, that there may be meat in mine house, and prove me now herewith, saith the LORD of hosts, if I will not open you the windows of heaven, and pour you out a blessing, that there shall not be room enough to receive it.*
11. *And I will rebuke the devourer for your sakes*

What is he saying? Starting in verse 8 he says a lot of our problems are because we haven't been doing what is right. What haven't we been doing right? We have been robbing God of what are rightfully His - His tithes and offerings, and therefore we are being cursed because of it.

And to correct this failure, we have to correct it by showing our faith and trust in Him by starting to do what we're supposed to do. And if we do what He tells us, He will give us back far more than we gave Him. So much more that you will not have room for it all. Wow, what a promise!

(First of all, remember, as one of God's laws, it had been around from the beginning of time on this earth. We just haven't heard much about it because that was one of the many things that had slipped out of the scriptures when his scribes tried to put the Bible together for King James. And it seems it might have been done a little differently back then too, But thankfully Malachi was there to come to the rescue.)

But wait, what was that important thing that he said? This is one of those laws of God that doesn't logically calculate in our mortal minds. How can you get more than you already have by giving away part of what little you have to begin with?

You don't have to try to figure it out; there is no rational way we can come up with that answer. As a mathematician most of my life, at least as a person who worked with and depends on numbers to do so much of what I have done for many years I always believed numbers don't lie. Well they don't, but they also don't necessarily calculate logically when it comes to trying to figure out tithing. Because this says, by having faith in him, you can get more out of ten when you first take one away from it.

But that isn't all. Sometimes we think, "I don't have time to do that - I'm already too busy to take on something else." Time works much like tithing. If we spend time doing something good for God and someone else, He will bless us with more time than we had to begin with, for getting our own things done.

Sound impossible? Yes!

Does it work? Prove it to yourself, but do it with faith, fearing nothing, trusting and believing in him, as it says *"prove me now herewith, saith the Lord of hosts, if I will not open you the windows of heaven, and pour you out a blessing."* (Malachi 3:10)

It is one of God's laws, and He does not lie, *"Yea, Lord, I know that thou speakest the truth, for thou art a God of truth, and canst not lie."* (Ether 3:10)

It does take faith, a lot of faith sometimes, especially when you are already down to your very last … - whatever. Sometimes we have to be brought down to the bottom before we can start going up again, and sometimes that is what it takes to strip our minds of its logic and start depending on Him, when we just can't do it for ourselves anymore.

If there were no drops of water, there would be no oceans. If there were no grains of sand, there would be no beach. If there were no atoms, there would be nothing to build a world with. And if there were no **you**, there would be no family of God, or reason for this life.

We need to realize we are absolutely nothing compared to the whole realm of things, but yet, **you** are a child of **God**, greater than the earth we live on, someone special that **He** knows and loves.

14-May-2003

GOD'S LAWS ARE ETERNAL

For every right there is a wrong, for every good there is a bad – there is opposition in all things. That is how we learn right from wrong, and we need to understand and be aware of this fact. We need to discern between the two, and always pick the good - if we can - to train the Spirit, and strengthen the body. What is important to know is that your reason for being here is to train the mind (your spirit) how to control your body to do what is right and it needs to do. This is one of the most important things we are here on this earth for, to train the Spirit how to cope with a body, since the spirit never had one before it came here (as a Spirit.) – And at the same time, teach the spirit all that is right, and to learn how to always do good things, rather than the bad.

There is an endless multitude of things God has created for us to utilize in this life to accomplish the tasks we have before us. And there are a multitude of things for us to learn, however, we are mere mortals, still learning how to get from one week to the next or even from one day to the next. So we need inspiration from the Holy Ghost and the scriptures to enlighten us.

Unfortunately, we often seem to be incapable of grasping more than one or two things at a time. And when we find something that doesn't seem to work for us, we might try to invent something unnatural to take care of the problem, or we might have a tendency to try to exclude it from everyone else, as well as ourselves – convinced that, if it doesn't work for me, it can't work for them either. (This is a tool used by the opposition to hide truths we might discover, and want to share, but instead, he tries to encourage us to fail.)

The same often goes with natural practitioners of healing. They might use different techniques and methods to arrive at the same place, and end up getting the same results, but want to selfishly discredit everyone else for doing it a different way, because it is not their way. And in so doing, may prevent someone from getting help from the other method.

Man's ideas are not infallible or flawless, no matter how much education you obtain, only God and His laws are perfect, and only those are the important ones when we leave this existence - for they are right and they are eternal.

His laws are so encompassing there is nothing we can even imagine that do not come within the rules He has already laid out for us. So we shouldn't even try to ignore what is right, or fight against something that is correct, and works. There is room for all kinds of differences here, as long as they all follow God's rules – allow them to be, learn from them, and give those differences a chance to grow.

Since the mind isn't used as much as it should be, it sometimes has a tendency to shut down before it wants to grasp something new; it gets weak, and loses strength. However, by using it, perhaps creatively, you can accomplish amazing things. And just like the muscles in your arms and legs get stronger with use, so does the brain.

Actually, some of those incorrect outside influences, through various means, including deception, temptation, and dishonest trickery can do what may look like the same good things – but only for the ultimate purpose of undermining, tearing down, and destroying, rather than building, strengthening, and improving, so this must constantly be guarded against. And any good they might appear to provide, is very short lived.

This is another reason we need to be guided by the inspiration of the Holy Ghost, and the reason we need to be sure to keep a clear head, uninfluenced by something, such as narcotics, drugs or anything that is unnatural or harmful to the body, like alcohol, smoking, etc.. And a good reason to practice deep meditation and training of the mind, along with sincere prayer. To learn what the body needs, and to do things in a productive way. That prevents those backward outside forces from influencing the mind and body in the wrong direction.

Just as a side note, the earth on which we live is also a living body, just as we are; it's just in a different form than we usually think of as being an individual entity. You might play with the idea. Think of the trees and plants on the earth as the hair on your head; and the grass as your whiskers (if you're a man.) And just as we have a high percentage of water in us, so does the earth, it's just more obvious on the earth, than it is in us.

The expression "Mother Earth" is often used, and for good reason, since the earth is the supplier of most everything we are made of, and we need in our mortal lives. For instance, the herbs, food, and fruits we use for proper nutrition, and in turn, the oxygen those things produce for us.

That of course, isn't **totally** true. We absolutely need the energies provided by the Sun, as well as the physical influences provided by all the other heavenly bodies circling around within our universe. But if the earth becomes sick through our uncaring stupid pollutions, it has a difficult time of providing us with everything we need, and in helping keep us healthy.

For our selfish sakes, we need to keep the earth clean and strong so it can supply all the things we need to survive. Fortunately, God has given the earth a great ability to correct its own needs, and recover and renew itself from all the ills mankind has thrust upon it. This is a loving God who watches out for us. It is mankind that doesn't.

Our own bodies are amazing machines that can also recover from ills we ourselves cause to come upon us, if we allow them to heal. The ancient art called Homeopathy can actually help **cure** many of these difficulties by encouraging the body to do just that. Hippocrates talked about it in the fourth century BC. It has more documented proof and success in healing than the drugs of today's medical profession that seem to destroy more lives than they are saving, because for the most part, drugs are only "*treating symptoms*" rather than "*curing illnesses*" – by essentially using man-made chemicals, to send sicknesses deep underground where they can hide, smolder, and fester until they have gained enough power to completely destroy their host.

How ironic, since Hippocrates, known as "the father of Medicine" is also the one who is given credit for the doctor's "Hippocratic oath" which is supposed to guarantee that a doctor is to first, "do no harm." Don't get me wrong, if I break a leg or something, I will be looking for a good doctor to take care of that sort of thing.

In the earth's creation, God provided most all things we generally need to survive, for as long as we are required to live on it. And each of these things needs the other, for the benefit of the whole. The world is designed to constantly renew itself for as long as is necessary for us to complete our tasks here, and furnish every physical need we have and require of it. However, when mankind starts interfering, changing, modifying, inventing, and manipulating what God has provided, into something unnatural - probably most likely for monetary gain, that is when things start going haywire and downhill. Not necessarily, that *some* of these things are wrong, but that they need to be done in the proper way.

Fears of depletion and shortage are also just man's contrivances and imaginations, caused by those opposing forces that want you to believe God is dead, or not smart enough to know how to take care of His world, or do what is right, and that He is not the greatest of all beings. If we don't understand these simple lies, than perhaps we deserve to be deceived and fear, but no one has the right to try to force those ideas on others.

Many other things on and in the earth are also suppliers of the energies we can utilize. For instance, crystals have the ability to focus certain minute energies in a way that they can supply certain strengths to our systems. And they can help draw out illnesses, to allow the body to heal itself. Different crystals are made of different materials, in different ways, and consequently, they have different wave lengths and energies, and logically these energies influence different systems and organs when used for healing purposes.

Speaking of subtle minuscule energies, Feng Shui, the placement, direction, and utilization of different article's energies when positioned purposefully can be used to concentrate, direct, channel, balance, and focus energies even in seemly inanimate objects, to benefit and influence the body and spirit of a person, such as even the chair you sit in, or the bed you sleep in, if done correctly.

Even the scent of flowers, have an influence on our systems. This is called Aromatherapy by those who study this science. We, as a people, like the pleasant smells, but they also influence the mind and body when considering health. For instance, the scent of Lavender can increase mental alertness, or have a calming effect on agitated behavior – and Jasmine next to your bed can help fight depression. "Essential oils," are likewise beneficial to us for these same reasons, for their scent and beneficial remedial effects. These things are god's gifts to us.

Fats are also needed for a healthy body, in spite of what we are often told, without them we would not be able to live a healthy life, and can even die. But of course, like all things, too much of any one thing can also be too much. Moderation is an important rule to remember in all things.

Even colors can have an influence on our minds and bodies, and should be utilized rather than ridiculed or ignored. Hopefully this treatise, along with the one entitled "According to the Law," will enlighten those who read them, so they will begin to understand God is in all things, and we should give him credit for all this fantastic, and amazing creation, for his greatness and total understanding of all things. And to know that **all** things are a part of the whole and when used according to **His** will, it will be, for **our** good.

If we would only stop fighting amongst ourselves about who is right or wrong, or better than someone else, or has more of something, or for any other reason - perhaps we could use the little bit of knowledge we have, or obtain, to figure things out better for ourselves, and it would benefit all mankind.

Once all these things are taken into consideration, the importance of getting the body adequately supplied with good nutrition and oxygen might have been the focus here, but there is so much more to learn and know – and it is up to us to learn all we can. Simply ask, and have **faith** to receive it.

I don't claim to have anywhere near enough knowledge to explain all these things myself, I would be a fool to imply as much, but I do see that we need to grasp a hold of as much truth as we can.

Only time will tell what all God has for us. I know He has given us far more than we realize. It would be well if we would tell Him, "Thank You," and ask that He guide us in all things. That simple phrase, "*Thank you,*" would help us find, and understand even more things to help us live a better life while upon this earth. And, if you acknowledge Him, He will do the same for you, and give you additional help – so don't forget to thank Him for **<u>all</u>** things.

I testify that God lives, that this world, and everything in, on, under, and over it are His creation, and He has allowed us to come here for a moment in time to learn just as much as we possibly can. We need only to consider all things that are right and good, and then try to exclude ourselves from all things that aren't.

20-Feb-2010

INVESTING IN LIFE

Investing in the stock market is often sort of like betting on the old nag in the third race. Theoretically, investing indicates someone has investigated the soundness of the investment, trying; through study, examination, and calculation, to predict the possibility that something is going to work out, and in the long run pays off in the end, getting something better back, and more than you put into it. We're not prophets, knowing what is coming, but we can determine somewhat what we'd like to happen. So, what do you want to get out of your investment in life?

Marriage is an investment in life. Theoretically, in picking a spouse, you logically should investigate the soundness of the investment, and its purpose is to end up with getting the most out of your investment, and not just dumping your valuables down a rat hole. Typically, earthly marriage in this life is good, but is only one step away from "shacking-up", which is Satan's way of trying to get something for nothing.

Even in most marriages there has been little or no investigating into the soundness of the deal, and no real love has been exercised or lost. Perhaps only infatuation and lust has prompted the deal. It is the reason that for every three or four marriages, only one might last for more than a short time. The thrill of the ride lasts only for a moment.

And bouncing from one to another in marriage is perhaps just as bad as shacking up. The scriptures have much to say about this, and divorce in general. So if you are concerned about what the Bible says about it and your place in God's Kingdom, you might want to check it out. Marriage though is good and should be your goal, if done properly. But if you don't do it properly, then there is much to be lost.

In the mean time, the inevitable happens. New life is brought into the world and then discarded and dumped on the street like a mongrel dog. It happens far too often. Love is more than lust, it is a commitment. Love is something of substance, something that should last forever, through thick and thin, that doesn't fade, but becomes stronger as it matures, not something that can be used and then thrown away when the newness wears off. What is your commitment to the investment going to be when you invest in life – or in theirs? And the children you bring into this life?

Are you dedicated to stick with the investment you made for the rest of your mortal life? Or are you only seeing the exterior layer of someone who appears to be new and different, that might soon rust and become worthless in your eyes?

If you are dedicated to making things work, even when the newness has lost its shine, and you become partners for life, you have only taken one little step away from "shacking up." Marriage is that first step, but hopefully, that investment includes something more; providing everything you possibly can to fulfill all the requirements of your partner – not just in things, or stuff, which have no real value, but in feelings, hopes, and love unfeigned. If that is the case and maturity starts with a bond of marriage where you two can become truly one; that is very good.

But what's going to happen when you are ripped apart by death of one or the other? The scriptures say, ". . *if a man marry him a wife in the world, and he marry her not by me nor by my word, and he covenant with her so long as he is in the world and she with him, their covenant and marriage are not of force when they are dead*". (D&C 132:15) Wow, did you get that?

When you marry "in the world", it is exactly as it says in the marriage vows, "till death do you part"! What if your partner dies?

Until that actually happens you will never know how really terrible that can be, but when it does, what then? You will never see your partner again. – How tragic. – Is it really worth it?

Yes it is, if you will do one more thing to guarantee that that separation never happens. Remember, marriage (in this life) is only for this life, "*until death do you part*".

Your investment was not good for the long haul. You have lost all your precious invested time and efforts – but if you take one more step farther away from shacking up, your investment will provide you with everlasting unity, happiness and peace. That one more step requires that you go to the Temple of the Lord, and be *sealed* together for time and for all of eternity, and indicates your real commitment is doing everything you can that is exactly correct. "*. . verily I say unto you, if a man marry a wife by my word, which is my law, and by the new and everlasting covenant, and it is sealed unto them by the Holy Spirit of promise, by him who is anointed, unto whom I have appointed this power and the keys of this priesthood; and it shall be said unto them—Ye shall come forth in the first resurrection; … and shall inherit thrones, kingdoms, principalities, and powers, dominions, all heights and depths… in time, and through all eternity; and shall be of full force when they are out of the world; and they shall pass by the angels, and the gods, which are set there, to their exaltation and glory in all things, as hath been sealed upon their heads, which glory shall be a fulness and a continuation of the seeds forever and ever." (D&C 132:19)* Then that separation will never come, it will be a union forever.

Your investment will then be fully protected and all the effort you have put into its successful maturity will pay off in untold value with an endless fountain of prosperity. Are you willing to take that extra, extremely important step, or do you just want to shack-up – and lose everything?

20-Oct-2009

ARE YOU FULL OF ENERGY?

That probably all depends on how you look at things. If someone says, you are full of it. That usually isn't what they are referring to. And if you have been around for *a number of years*, more than likely there are times when you don't always have quite as much bounce in your step as you once did. That is understandable if you've got a few miles on the old chassis. No matter how much time you spend on vehicle maintenance, or hours you spend in front of the mirror keeping the body polished, we live in a temporary world where things are constantly changing, and naturally deteriorating. No matter how diligent you are in keeping things in good working order, you just can't keep the buggy going forever.

Can you imagine the traffic jams we'd have if nothing went to the scrap heap, and you just kept adding more and more bodies to the picture? As much as a long life sounds good, that's not the kind of place where I'd really want to live. It'd be too crowded to move around.

In spite of the fact we are made up of 60 to 70% water, as they say, we still take up a lot of space. But even if you were to squeeze out all that liquid, all the chemicals that would be left that we're made of, would only add up to a few measly dollars, even at the inflated price of our modern currency. And no matter how fat you get, all that bulk still wouldn't add more than a few pennies to your worth - looking at it simply from a material point of value.

Isn't it great to know that there is a God watching over us, And He values us much differently? Remember, *the worth of souls is **great** in the sight of God.* (D&C 18:10)

But let's look at this still a different way. If you were to look, with a high powered microscope, at how the physical body is made, you would see we are made up of millions of tiny little atoms. Each one of those atoms is made up of a multitude of other bits and pieces, just how many, nobody even knows yet. And in-between all those tiny bits and pieces is enormous amounts of space (relatively speaking.) But even that space isn't all by itself. That space is just crammed full of energy. It's what is keeping all those bits and pieces in their proper places. And if your microscope was powerful enough, you could see all those bits and pieces are constantly dancing around like they were just too excited to stand still, having a square dance you wouldn't believe.

That's why, even with all that space inside every atom, and filling you up with more space than any solid substance, you can't just walk through something else. All that tremendous amount of energy in those spaces is preventing that from happening. So, looking at it from that perspective, yes, you are full of more energy than anything else. And no matter how smart any of us get on this beautiful earth, none of us will ever get smart enough to make a real duplicate of you, or know how it's all done. You are unique, a one of a kind.

All that energy bottled up inside of you has other attributes too, besides just holding you all together. Even though it's all pretty well contained, its influence can be felt by someone else, even if they're not right up next to you. Yes again, it's very subtle, and may not be very strong, but it is there. And even though we may not be openly aware of it, we are influenced by it.

The ancients, those cultures and civilizations that have existed the longest on the earth, that were not being bombarded with electronic gadgets and could still think, had time to realize some of these things and figure out how these tiny energy influences could be used for their benefit.

They realized that all things, even what we would call inanimate things, like a chair, table, wall, everything, has these subtle energies because everything is made up of the same kind of atoms with all that energy buzzing around inside of them. They probably didn't know about the atom, or how things are made with all their little bits and pieces whizzing around in space, but they recognized the influences they had on other things, and people around them. And they used what they knew to make things better. I also need to mention here, they didn't have TV commercials either, constantly pumping copious amounts of rubbish, garbage, litter and lies into their ears and eyes.

Unfortunately, even with all the learning, and understanding we have come to realize, we have at the same time lost so much of the real knowledge that people once had, that we are probably going backward faster than we are progressing and going forward.

Just as our chassis is slowly rusting away, so goes the brain cells. Progress can only be made if we learn from, and keep, all the knowledge we learn, and add to it. We will never succeed if every time we learn something new, we throw away something we had already learned before. That's like sliding back a step and a half for every two we take forward - like trying to go up a hill of sand. We might eventually get to the top if we keep struggling away and working at it, if we don't get exhausted and give up on the way, but I don't bet on something that's not a sure thing, and that's not betting.

If you take these things into account, what is happening to every new generation of children that comes into this world? Unfortunately they are the ones losing out, that will never learn all that they should be. Is this why this world is going to Hell?

So what is the purpose of this paper that talks about something that any thinking person already knows, or really doesn't care about? I would like to suggest that, first of all, we recognize God. He put all things together. He is the only one who knows how everything works. We need to learn what He has for us, and all that He gives us.

Unfortunately, as mankind has learned a thing or two, the first thing mankind has done, is think he has become smarter than God, and therefore that is the first truth he has thrown away instead of build on it. Consequently, mankind is already going backward, instead of forward.

So first of all, we **must** remember and recognize God. Learn of Him, and what He has done for us. And I must add, continues to do for us every single moment of every single measure of time. Then, learn why we are here. Why has God placed us here on this earth? For what purpose?

What are we supposed to be learning from this temporary existence? And what are we supposed to do while we are here?

It is obvious this is not what anyone wants to hear! As soon as God is mentioned, things in your head and mind want to shut it out, back away, and throw this paper away! You actually want to resist listening to what it might say here, or go any farther. That is the second truth you need to learn.

In spite of the truth that God exists, there is also an opposing force that also exists, who wants to repel that first truth, who wants to completely obliterate that fact.

That brings us to truth number three. There is truth (which is God), and there is false (which is trying to tell you there is no God), and then there is choice. You have your choice to choose which you will believe in. If you choose to not believe in God, that doesn't change the fact that, whether you believe it or not, there *is* a God!

You can still believe something else if that's what you want to believe. But if you want to believe that, than you must also rule out the idea of ever receiving any good from Him, or any help from Him, or …, well anything. But you still have your freewill to choose for yourself. That is a gift to you from God. It is your choice.

From here, you have your entire earthly life to learn anything you want. There are many choices to make, and a multitude of things to learn; far more than any of us can even imagine. New things are being learned every day. But what you really shouldn't want to do is forget, or throw away anything good you have already learned. Don't take a step in the sand, build on that firm solid footing of the truth you have already learned and climb from there.

That brings us full circle; back around to those subtle energies I was talking about. These are truths to learn from, to benefit from, to grow from, and to use for gaining more knowledge. So what can we, and should we, learn about, and from, about these subtle energies?

If we recognize them, knowing in our mind that they exist, whether we feel them or not, we can use them to build on. Stack them up perhaps, figuratively at least, to make them stronger so we can benefit from them even more than by themselves. This is where we need to go back to learn from the ancients, because it takes too long to learn it all for ourselves. It took them hundreds, if not thousands, of years to learn what they've learned, and figure out how to use it.

If I were rich, and could, I would like to start from scratch, building my home exactly how, and with what I wanted, to gain the greatest benefit. That is not possible for me, and even if it were, things are not static. As mentioned, things are constantly changing. This is a temporary world, which we have little control over, so all we can do here, is the best we can do.

But if I could, first of all, I would search out all I could learn from the ancients, utilizing their gained wisdom about how I would prepare the ground; how to face the house, how to lay it out, and build it for the best benefit. Then, but actually starting with its design, I would furnish it with all the proper items, and place them in the proper way to strengthen their combined energies.

Even then, in this temporary world I would have to recognize that things would change beyond my control. So I would have to regularly modify, move, or replace things to try to maintain the ideal energy I wished for. I guess you could say that is another attribute of a temporary world; we are not here to sit back on our behind and do nothing, we have to constantly work at it.

This is the same way we need to think about our life, and that of our children. They are more important than a house. "Position" them properly for their best benefit, and all things around them. Continue to modify and add to whatever is necessary to strengthen them.

But beyond that, I would never forget my God, and recognize that He is over all good things, and whatever I did would have to be in harmony with Him if I wanted it to be right, and correct, and good. That would be my ultimate goal. To gain the perfection I was striving for, to constantly search for all the good things that I could, to keep building on what I've learned, and adding more and more to it every day of my life until I had received as much as I was able to achieve – and doing the same for my children.

And that is the way I need to approach life and the scriptures. There is far more wisdom stuffed into those few words given to help me learn from, that it is almost mind boggling. I need to look to the prophets to help me learn all they have come to understand. To recognize that in God's kingdom that all things have been learned, all truth is there.

And if I am able to learn from them and understand what is contained in the scripture is not only true, all those truths are unchanging. They never have changed, and never will. They are always true, and always have been, no matter how confused the world has become. If I learn all these things, and don't deviate from them, then I am building my house, and family to never fail. Only mortality is variable.

Eventually, when our time has been fulfilled with this existence, and we are allowed to go back home where God resides, perhaps then we will have a chance to rest from our labors – but more than likely by then we will be so full of energy and have gotten so used to working hard that we'll want to just keep going, and do more and more of all the good things we've learned to do, and we'll even have the energy to do it all. It is my belief, that the more good we are able to do here, the greater will be whatever comes next! May each of us learn all we can, constantly building on every good thing we have already learned, and be so full of energy there will be no desire to just sit back and do nothing!

5-Jan-2011

ARE YOU PERFECT?

God could have made us perfect, or we could do it on our own, but we aren't likely to live that long, or supposed to live forever in this life. Who in their right mind would want to live that long in this corrupted world? Besides, this world is already getting to be too crowded to be enjoyable, can you imagine what it would be like if no one ever died? Actually we came here temporarily, and to (hopefully) try to make ourselves perfect before we move on. At least do everything we can to become more perfect before we are taken from the earth.

We have been sent here, to this little blue rock, just long enough to learn how to be good children of our Father in Heaven. I hope I am learning all that He wants me to, and will have learned all I need to before I have to leave and go on to the next step in life. God is more perfect than any of us can even imagine, and has greater love for all of us, and all things, than our tiny mortal minds can possibly understand at this point in our perfection. In contrast to him, most of us are a very long way from becoming perfect yet.

But being like Him is what we need to be trying to learn while we are here. Most of the distractions that fill this world seem to be designed to keep us from ever doing that, and learning what we were sent here to do. But that is the objective for coming here, to learn and to refine ourselves so we can eventually become perfect. That seems to be very difficult to do, but even with our daily work that we have to do, we can still work on God's plan and even have some time to enjoy this life - if we just will.

This idea of becoming perfect is so important; God's specially commissioned Son came to this earth to specifically tell us about his Father's master plan; and what we need to do to be like Him. The Son actually gave His own mortal life to emphasize it and show us that it can be done. Were you listening to what He had to say, and what He told us?

It was also so important, His Prophets, and their scribes, wrote down most of what He said while he was here so we had a record of what He told us we should be doing. Those records were accumulated into several books and in some cases; those books were combined into larger books. There are at least five books of books called Scriptures that I know of at this time, and everyone of them are just as important as the others. So they should all be studied.

Isn't that wonderful that we have them now so we can read and review them regularly when we forget what He said. How long has it been since you read those things? If you're having problems of one kind or another, it might be that you need to read them again. Read them slowly, and carefully, ponder what you read so you can get the full meaning that is contained in them especially for you. Every time you read them, you will learn more.

Even before He came to live on the earth, the Son was talking to the Prophets, preparing them, and us, for when He would come, and now that He has been here and gone, He still talks to the Prophets in preparation for when He will come again. We better be prepared for that day, because He won't be coming as a little child this time, He will be coming as a great man of power and strength to make things right that we have been too ignorant, too lazy, or too wicked to do for ourselves. – And do the other things that only He can do.

Since God is "the same yesterday, today, and forever" as the Prophets tell us, we know that God has not changed, and neither has his Son. And the Prophets are still at work telling us everything we need to know, just like they have been doing for hundreds of years, so if He seems more distant to us than He did to the Prophets, it's probably because we have abandoned Him, not the other way around. And if we have abandoned Him, we better start embracing Him, because when that day comes, it will come very suddenly, and it will be both terrible and great, so we better be ready, and be on His side.

God, our Heavenly Father, is number one in our universe. His Son is number two (and the true God of this world), and the Holy Ghost is the third member of the "Godhead", and He is upon the earth even now, whispering truth in the ears of good people, who want to do what is right. He can do the same for you if you allow Him to. And if you want to always have Him with you, you can receive Him as a constant companion, if you follow God's rules. *"Ask, and it shall be given you; seek and ye shall find; knock and it shall be opened unto you: For every one that asketh receiveth; and he that seeketh findeth; and to him that knocketh, it shall be opened."* (Matt 7:8, Luke 11:10, 3 Nephi 14:8)

That means on your knees in humble prayer, and through that honest supplication, you will be led to the truth if you diligently search it out, or the truth will find you. **But, "be not deceived"**. (Luke 21:8) There are many who will try to convince you they know it all and what is right. Be very cautious, they may not even know what they are talking about. Search for the ones who have the whole truth and have the proper authority from the Son of God to make it available to you. If you sincerely desire to live in glory and in perfect harmony with your Father in Heaven and receive all His marvelous blessings beyond measure, pray for the proper teachings to be brought to you by the Elders of Jesus Christ's church, there is only one true way, and there is no deviation in His truth.

24-Jul-2009

ARE YOU AFRAID?

If you are, you're not along. Every time you listen to the radio or television, or pick up a newspaper, you hear of all the evil that is happening and bringing the world down around our ears. It is everywhere, no matter where in the world you might live. All the gangs, murders, rapes, abuse, persecution, torture, oppression, and every other type of evil that can be thought up by man (and Satan) is pervading the world. And that's just on the nightly TV programming.

Actually though, the TV shows are a real reflection and example of what is happening in the world today, and *maybe* not even as bad as real reality.

And no matter how many laws are passed and brought into play, things just continue to get worse and worse every day. In fact, the more laws that are passed it seems like they just make things worse instead of making them better. Why? Perhaps by trying to take away mans free agency and having to spell out every little iota of right, mankind doesn't know what is right any more without it being all written out in detail for them. But if that is the case, why aren't they even doing what is already written for everybody?

In fact, the more mankind tries to make things better, the worse things get. It seems the harder **mankind** tries to head in the right direction, the farther behind we get. The more people are given things the more they expect, and the more helpless they get.

Everybody wants everything handed to them freely without doing anything to earn it. Apparently they don't realize that someone has to pay for their things. What are they going to do when they find out they are going to end up having to pay for everything they've gotten?

Have you ever stopped to think maybe we're going about things all wrong? Maybe we need to start looking around at what's going on and start doing things differently.

First, we need to understand where we are, how we got where we are, and only then do we start to realize we probably need to be doing things differently – something we haven't been doing for a long, long time, instead of keeping on going down the same old path that just keeps getting us deeper and deeper into the mire we're already in. Otherwise, these "last days" before Jesus Christ comes again are going to get really rough.

Yes, Satan is surely at the heart of this, but our own stupidity is catching up awfully fast, so we can't blame it all on him.

The United States is known by the world as the "promised land," and rightfully so. People from all over the world have flocked here to have the freedoms and prosperity they crave. Yet, as soon as they get here, many of them start trying to make it into the same kind of messed up country they just came from, and in the process, this land no longer has any promise to be so special. Religious freedoms they never had where they came from, are likewise being perverted and being trampled underfoot.

And that is the most obvious thing that comes to mind. Ever since people started trying to shove God out of our society, bad things have just been getting worse and worse. The more God is shoved out into the cold, things have really started heating up, and the fires of Hell are not where I want to go.

A few rebel radicals who would rather follow Satan than God, are also screaming things like "discrimination" - and rather than "*offending*" anyone and standing up for what's right, and what made America great, our weak kneed society is bowing down to these anti-Christ's.

Through out the world's history this has happened several times. Do you remember hearing about a great flood that wiped an unrighteous people off the earth? Or the people of Sodom and Gomorrah who were so perverted God got rid of the whole bunch. Or the hundreds of thousands of the Tribe of Joseph who were allowed to be almost completely destroyed off the face of the earth because they turned away from God – just to name a few of the many times. How soon will it be before He decides none of us are worth keeping around any longer?

What we don't have to be afraid of is life, or afraid to believe in God; or His Son Jesus Christ who gave His life to save us from destruction, or be afraid of doing what the Holy Ghost tells us is really right. What we should be afraid of is turning away from them, and getting lazy and slothful.

You have your free agency, given to you by God to choose what you want to do, and to believe in. No one can take that gift away from you, that is God's gifts to you, and actually (*and this is the most wonderful and important part of this whole thing*) the more you believe in God, read the Scriptures, and do good things according to His counsel and guidance which comes through His Holy Prophets and the Holy Scriptures, the more good and prosperity you will have in this life – as long as you don't get proud and boastful of that prosperity, or put someone down because you think you are better than they are.

Check it out. Put it to the test. Read a little of the Scriptures every day so you know what they actually say, and don't forget to talk with your Father in Heaven about them in your daily prayers. If you live righteously He will hear, and listen, and help you with your problems if you are sincere – and you won't need to be afraid any longer, no matter how bad the world gets around you.

Yes, times are going to get rough, and many more bad things are going to be happening. And you will probably have to work harder than you ever have before, to keep your head in the right place, but when you are trying your best, and doing your best to be obedient to all of His commandments **He** will be proud of you, so **you** don't have to be. He will bless you abundantly, and He won't have any reason to think about getting rid of you.

Weather the storm, hold you head up high, do what is right and don't fear the one who really counts, and He will bless you abundantly for it. Just think what this world would be like if everyone did these things, and got on their knees just a couple times every day. We aren't afraid, let's start us a revolution, and do something good for somebody every day,

7-Jan-2010

ARE YOU GOOD ENOUGH?

Do you believe in God? Do you believe there is a God? Do you know there is a God? I believe there is a God. I believe that God is, and that He does exist – even though I don't really know there is a God.

I mean, I have never actually seen Him that I can remember. I have never actually met Him that I can remember. But yet I *do* believe in Him, and I *know* that He exists. If you just look around and see this amazing world we live in, and all the miracles it contains, it seems if you have any sense at all, you would have to realize and understand there is no way all these amazing things could just happen for no reason, without a plan, and with no forethought, and without *God*.

If all these things just happened by accident, then why are you so miserable and in the predicament you're in? Why have all those good "accidents" that must have taken place for all those millions of years, as some say must have happened to bring about all this "evolution" and prosperity and beauty, stopped at your doorstep?

I used to wonder, and be appalled, at how a third of the hosts of Heaven, a third of all my brothers and sisters that were created by Him, could turn away from our loving parents and deny they ever existed. Especially after having actually lived with them and actually knowing who they were.

Then one day, while reading the scriptures again, it dawned on me.

Even though God is God, and He does everything right because He is perfect – all the materials He made us out of must **not** have all been refined and purified and were not perfect.

Whatever those materials were, they are materials that existed somewhere forever, and are as random as every breath of air we breathe, and every atom we are made of here. Those were the raw materials He used to make us out of in our creation. The perfection had to come afterward, after we were formed, and that is what we are here for, to see if we are worth His efforts.

He has given us that opportunity, and the choice to make ourselves the best we want to be. That is up to us, we can be what **we** want to be. And yes, perfection of each one of us is possible, if we want it bad enough for ourselves, and if we would just do it, even though we were made from materials randomly dipped out of the vat of what was called intelligence.

We have learned that intelligence apparently has a different meaning than we usually give it. At least it isn't always as perfected as we have been led to believe, and can vary quite a bit in its original form. And as they say, you can't make a silk purse out of a sow's ear.

So, are we good enough? I don't believe I will ever be good enough here, although I also believe in trying to become that. That is the only way any of us are ever going to be good enough – by working hard and learning all we can, wherever we are, and doing whatever we are doing.

Yes, we have our choice to do whatever crazy thing we decide to do with what we have, and what we want to believe. If we want to believe the worst, the worst is what we will get. If we want to deny the truth, to us the truth is a lie. Look around, isn't that exactly what you see in those around you?

You see; those third of our brothers and sisters had their choice, like all of us, to believe as they wanted, and they chose to believe they were better than their own parents, and believed they themselves were so perfect already they didn't need any more perfection.

And they got exactly what they wanted. What they wanted was good enough, and that is all they are ever going to get. Because they were so adamant about it, they were separated out, and shut out from the next class in the road of development. That third had violated the eternal law of love and were thus stricken from ever getting more – and their progression stopped dead.

You and I, along with everyone else around us, could see a tiny bit further. We believed there was more to be had, and we got the chance to continue forward to see what we were really made of.

Unfortunately, many of us who wanted more, decided after they got here, that getting something better was a little harder to get than they wanted to give. They felt working for it was just too hard, and that just taking it from someone else was a lot easier. That sort of thing is also violating the eternal laws we must all live by. Somehow though, all of us here got past that first step first – but just barely – and some of them haven't gotten past that, or caught in their dishonesty, yet.

What is nice to know is that we are not all divided in separate individual boxes. We are an even spread deviating slightly from each other so minutely we are almost like the next, but not quite the same, and Father in Heaven knows the difference.

However, since we are all children of our Godly parents, we will all eventually be judged by those same divine, perfect laws they live. So we will each receive the reward (or punishment) we earn for ourselves, and not necessarily the same as what we think our neighbor should. But, our judgment will be just, true and perfect.

We are all in a gradient from good to bad. Meaning there are some almost as bad as those who never came here, and there are some who are so good they almost didn't need to come here. The important word here is "almost". And spread out in between these two extremes are all of us who have come here to improve our selves - or not, until we can earn the passing grade of perfection that will allow us to be numbered among those who are good enough to go on to get our passing grade and eventually earn our diploma. Or those that are just sent on anyway without learning anything.

So the question is; why can't we all just get along? The answer is, of course, there are those who just will not, and there are others who are not satisfied with anything, no matter how wonderful things are.

And for the rest of us, I guess that is good, because they show the rest of us how not to be, and of course then also, how to be.

Hopefully - you that are reading this - are one of us who wants to learn how to always do better, and are willing to learn and earn everything you can about being the best you can be.

So remember, God has achieved perfection, by his own work and struggles. And even though He is now perfect, the materials He made us out of were not perfect, but in our creation, He has given us the opportunity to become perfect even as He has done. Our perfection is not in our material make up, but in our own hands and what we make of ourselves. And in our so doing can earn those same rewards He has accomplished for Himself. Isn't that wonderful, and it should give us all hope.

How we can do that is laid out for us in the scriptures, which tell about Jesus, who is our brother, and who also had to do everything correctly to receive His glorification. He was the only one who never made any mistakes, meaning of course that all the rest of us have made at least one mistake - and more than likely, multitudes of them. - But if we accept this one perfect man as our example and allow Him to pay for our mistakes for us, if we earn that right, we can be judged as perfect as Him, and receive those same rewards as He has earned for Himself.

Being so good that He never made a mistake earned Him the right to be known as the Christ, who could then take away all the wrongs everyone else ever did wrong. And if we accept Him as our debt payer, and are obedient to following the laws He laid out for us, doing everything He tells us to do, then we will be found with that passing grade we need to continue on in our quest for progression and perfection. And we will understand that the difficulties we have here are for our own good, to help us learn how to overcome all difficulties, no matter how difficult they may seem at times, or become.

8-Nov-11

ABRAHAM

Everyone who professes to be a Christian, no matter what church they might belong to, or even if they don't read the scriptures, go to church, or profess to be a Christian - have probably heard of Abraham. More than likely, you, and they, are all descendants of Abraham.

Anyone with any sense knows that Adam was the first man in God's earthly creation of this world. What some may not understand is, he was one of the first steps in God's glorious plan to test His children. To see if they wanted to be good children, return to Him, and earn great rewards that would go with them (even after they died) into a never ending eternity. Which could be a place of wealth and prosperity, peace, happiness and glorious goodness, where there would never be death again, or despair, discouragement, sickness, sorrow or anything dark, dreary, bad or sad anymore.

Even if these people don't realize, or know, that the world got off to a really bad start and Satan took over causing turmoil, terror, chaos, and sin so rampant that God had to wash almost everyone off the earth with a great flood, leaving only eight people left on the earth. Yet they probably have heard about Abraham.

Much like Adam and Eve had done in the beginning; and Noah and his family had to do after the flood, Abraham was sort of like them, in that he was one of the first men in a long line of the multitudes of people that have lived on the earth. Adam and Eve were the first to "be fruitful and multiply, and replenish the earth" with children. Then later, Noah, his three sons, and their wives, who were the only people left after the great flood, had to start all over producing all the men and women to populate the earth again. (*AND God blessed Noah and his sons, and said unto them, Be fruitful, and multiply, and replenish the earth.* Gen. 9:1)

Abraham (who was one of Noah's descendants) wasn't the only one around at his time in history, but he was a very good man, and because he understood God and His plan, God promised Abraham that he would be a "father of many nations" of the earth. (Gen 17:4) (And here we are!)

At first, Abraham didn't think that could ever happen, he didn't have any children, and he and his wife were getting too old to have children. But God always keeps his promises, and when they were very old, Abraham and Sarah had a son named Isaac, who was to be the beginning of that great (hopefully righteous) posterity. But then – God told Abraham to sacrifice Isaac. Can you imagine that?

But in that moment when Abraham's obedience to his God was being tested to its ultimate, one of the greatest lessons we have ever been taught, unfolded.

Because of his great faith in God, Abraham understood that even if he were to give up his only son, or even give his **own life** in obedience to God's commandments, if that was what God wanted him to do, things would somehow still work out alright. That takes a lot of faith.

Satan tries to convince people of this same thing, but you have to know God, and Satan, to know the difference. If you don't, Satan will destroy you and everything you could ever hope to receive thereafter and forever more. – Killing is never right, unless God commands it. And it is very unlikely that you would be anyone He would tell to do that – So don't even think about it!

However, if you are obedient to God, who is the one and only eternal Father in Heaven, even if you were to lose your life in doing what is right, and gave it standing up for Him, you will live again, and will still receive the blessings He has for you. Obedience to Him is the important principle we all need to learn.

God wishes every man could learn this. Abraham knew it - so he didn't actually have to sacrifice his son. And from that example, we learn that if we are asked to sacrifice our time and our talents, our interests, our safety, welfare or anything else we think of as our earthly valuables, be they monetary, time or anything else in this world, including our very life - in the end we will receive the rewards He has for us for having been obedient to Him.

This is why the world needs to remember Abraham. This is what we need to learn from Abraham. This is why God gave us Abraham, and used him to teach us this lesson. Learn well this lesson of **faith**, and **obedience** to *His commandments*. Thrust in your efforts and do the work of the Lord, and reap the harvest God has prepared for you in His eternal fields of glory where you shall dwell in eternity basking in that peace and happiness that waits for you.

2-Feb-2010

DIRECT QUOTE FROM THE SCRIPTURES

AND now, I speak also concerning those who do not believe in Christ. Behold, will ye believe in the day of your visitation—behold, when the Lord shall come, yea, even that great day when the earth shall be rolled together as a scroll, and the elements shall melt with fervent heat, yea, in that great day when ye shall be brought to stand before the Lamb of God—then will ye say that there is no God?

Then will ye longer deny the Christ, or can ye behold the Lamb of God? Do ye suppose that ye shall dwell with him under a consciousness of your guilt? Do ye suppose that ye could be happy to dwell with that holy Being, when your souls are racked with a consciousness of guilt that ye have ever abused his laws?

Behold, I say unto you that ye would be more miserable to dwell with a holy and just God, under a consciousness of your filthiness before him, than ye would to dwell with the damned souls in hell. For behold, when ye shall be brought to see your nakedness before God, and also the glory of God, and the holiness of Jesus Christ, it will kindle a flame of unquenchable fire upon you.

O then ye unbelieving, turn ye unto the Lord; cry mightily unto the Father in the name of Jesus, that perhaps ye may be found spotless, pure, fair, and white, having been cleansed by the blood of the Lamb, at that great and last day. And again I speak unto you who deny the revelations of God, and say that they are done away, that there are no revelations, nor prophecies, nor gifts, nor healing, nor speaking with tongues, and the interpretation of tongues;

Behold I say unto you, he that denieth these things knoweth not the gospel of Christ; yea, he has not read the scriptures; if so, he does not understand them. For do we not read that God is the same yesterday, today, and forever, and in him there is no variableness neither shadow of changing? And now, if ye have imagined up unto yourselves a god who doth vary, and in whom there is shadow of changing, then have ye imagined up unto yourselves a god who is not a God of miracles.

But behold, I will show unto you a God of miracles, even the God of Abraham, and the God of Isaac, and the God of Jacob; and it is that same God who created the heavens and the earth, and all things that in them are. Behold, he created Adam, and by Adam came the fall of man. And because of the fall of man came Jesus Christ, even the Father and the Son; and because of Jesus Christ came the redemption of man.

And because of the redemption of man, which came by Jesus Christ, they are brought back into the presence of the Lord; yea, this is wherein all men are redeemed, because the death of Christ bringeth to pass the resurrection, which bringeth to pass a redemption from an endless sleep, from which sleep all men shall be awakened by the power of God when the trump shall sound; and they shall come forth, both small and great, and all shall stand before his bar, being redeemed and loosed from this eternal band of death, which death is a temporal death.

And then cometh the judgment of the Holy One upon them; and then cometh the time that he that is filthy shall be filthy still; and he that is righteous shall be righteous still; he that is happy shall be happy still; and he that is unhappy shall be unhappy still.

And now, O all ye that have imagined up unto yourselves a god who can do no miracles, I would ask of you, have all these things passed, of which I have spoken? Has the end come yet? Behold I say unto you, Nay; and God has not ceased to be a God of miracles. Behold, are not the things that God hath wrought marvelous in our eyes? Yea, and who can comprehend the marvelous works of God? Who shall say that it was not a miracle that by his word the heaven and the earth should be; and by the power of his word man was created of the dust of the earth; and by the power of his word have miracles been wrought? And who shall say that Jesus Christ did not do many mighty miracles? And there were many mighty miracles wrought by the hands of the apostles.

And if there were miracles wrought then, why has God ceased to be a God of miracles and yet be an unchangeable Being? And behold, I say unto you he changeth not; if so he would cease to be God; and he ceaseth not to be God, and is a God of miracles.

And the reason why he ceaseth to do miracles among the children of men is because that they dwindle in unbelief, and depart from the right way, and know not the God in whom they should trust.

Behold, I say unto you that whoso believeth in Christ, doubting nothing, whatsoever he shall ask the Father in the name of Christ it shall be granted him; and this promise is unto all, even unto the ends of the earth.

For behold, thus said Jesus Christ, the Son of God, unto his disciples who should tarry, yea, and also to all his disciples, in the hearing of the multitude: Go ye into all the world, and preach the gospel to every creature; And he that believeth and is baptized shall be saved, but he that believeth not shall be damned;

And these signs shall follow them that believe—in my name shall they cast out devils; they shall speak with new tongues; they shall take up serpents; and if they drink any deadly thing it shall not hurt them; they shall lay hands on the sick and they shall recover;

And whosoever shall believe in my name, doubting nothing, unto him will I confirm all my words, even unto the ends of the earth.

And now, behold, who can stand against the works of the Lord? Who can deny his sayings? Who will rise up against the almighty power of the Lord? Who will despise the works of the Lord? Who will despise the children of Christ? Behold, all ye who are despisers of the works of the Lord, for ye shall wonder and perish.

O then despise not, and wonder not, but hearken unto the words of the Lord, and ask the Father in the name of Jesus for what things soever ye shall stand in need. Doubt not, but be believing, and begin as in times of old, and come unto the Lord with all your heart, and work out your own salvation with fear and trembling before him.

Be wise in the days of your probation; strip yourselves of all uncleanness; ask not, that ye may consume it on your lusts, but ask with a firmness unshaken, that ye will yield to no temptation, but that ye will serve the true and living God.

See that ye are not baptized unworthily; see that ye partake not of the sacrament of Christ unworthily; but see that ye do all things in worthiness, and do it in the name of Jesus Christ, the Son of the living God; and if ye do this, and endure to the end, ye will in nowise be cast out.

Behold, I speak unto you as though I spake from the dead; for I know that ye shall have my words. Condemn me not because of mine imperfection, neither my father, because of his imperfection, neither them who have written before him; but rather give thanks unto God that he hath made manifest unto you our imperfections, that ye may learn to be more wise than we have been.

And now, behold, we have written this record according to our knowledge, in the characters which are called among us the reformed Egyptian, being handed down and altered by us, according to our manner of speech. And if our plates had been sufficiently large we should have written in Hebrew; but the Hebrew hath been altered by us also; and if we could have written in Hebrew, behold, ye would have had no imperfection in our record.

But the Lord knoweth the things which we have written, and also that none other people knoweth our language; and because that none other people knoweth our language, therefore he hath prepared means for the interpretation thereof. And these things are written that we may rid our garments of the blood of our brethren, who have dwindled in unbelief. And behold, these things which we have desired concerning our brethren, yea, even their restoration to the knowledge of Christ, are according to the prayers of all the saints who have dwelt in the land.

And may the Lord Jesus Christ grant that their prayers may be answered according to their faith; and may God the Father remember the covenant which he hath made with the house of Israel; and may he bless them forever, through faith on the name of Jesus Christ. Amen.

Many, many years ago

THE BOOK OF MOSES

Moses was one of the great Prophets that lived in ancient times (though not real ancient, he wasn't born until the world had already been populated by Adam and Eve, and their children's children for more than **two thousand** years.) That means a lot of things had already been happening before he came along. But being a great man, and one of the great Prophets of this world, he knew there were a lot of things that had happened that we needed to know about.

Like the city of Enoch being taken into Heaven, the flood where all but 8 people were destroyed off the face of the earth, the dividing of the land into separate continents, and the life and times of Abraham, and the re-populating of the whole earth with all of Abraham's and Jacob's posterity.

Of course, he wasn't the first one to write things down. There was Adam, Seth, Jared, Enoch, and Noah just to name a few in the first thousand years, and a multitude of others that came along after the flood before Moses showed up, including the great Abraham. I'm sure every one of these many un-numbered great Prophets wrote things down pertaining to their own dispensation of time, and restored the truth each time it became corrupted. For instance, we know for a fact, after the flood, Noah had to start all over teaching their posterity all the things God wanted them to know and understand, just like Adam and Eve had to do from the beginning.[1] And where do you suppose Moses

---

1   Genesis 9:1 "AND God blessed Noah and his sons, and said unto them, Be fruitful, and multiply, and replenish the earth."

learned about everything these other Prophets and the people had gone through? He read all their histories himself.

Thankfully, Moses had, or was able to gather up, many of those records that had been written, and compiled and condensed them into what we call the Pentateuch, or what we might even call, "The Book of Moses." There were, of course, many things which he didn't, and couldn't write about in the 5 books he wrote that we now have in the Bible. And that's good. Can you imagine lugging all that with you when you went to Church every Sunday? He tried to give us the high-lights though, and the important *laws* his people needed to understand.

Unfortunately, some of the most important things that he wrote down were lost and weren't even included when they combined all the different books into a Bible² for King James back in the early 1600's. That was probably close to 4000 years after Moses' time, we're lucky even more of those very important things weren't lost.

Father in Heaven, being a very wise and intelligent God, knew the importance of those things Moses wrote that didn't get in the Bible though, and He saw to it that they weren't *all* lost and gone forever.

In the mean time, the "Brethren" put together the Bible for King James, including many of the manuscripts they thought were important, written by many of the other Prophets following Moses' time, including Malachi's, and Isaiah's, and called it the "**Old** Testament." All these were important too, and good ones.

Then they did the same with the records written by the Prophets that lived in the "Holy Land" during the time following the birth of Jesus Christ, up until the martyrdom of Him and all of His twelve Apostles. The time after that then became what is known as the "Dark Ages," when God's authority was withdrawn and withheld from the people, because of their evil and wicked actions.

The accumulation of those records was called the "**New** Testament."³ The records in the Bible of both these two eras are not in order of when

---

2   "Bible" is an ancient word meaning "the books" or "book of books."

3   Another meaning of the word "Testament," as used in the scriptures is, "Covenant" (Bible Dictionary), and the gospel is so arranged that principles and ordinances are received by covenant placing the recipient under strong obligation and responsibility to honor the commitment. You can take that as a warning to be obedient to the covenants, or testaments.

they were written, so that can be somewhat confusing at times, but we are still glad we have all that we have.

Actually, it really doesn't make any difference when any of them were written; all of the information in all of the books of the Bible is still just as valid as it ever was, even though some of those laws had been *fulfilled* by Jesus when He came to live on the earth.

But since some things had been fulfilled and it was also a new era, there were new ways of doing some things. For instance, the Gentiles could now be taught about, and be baptized into the Church, whereas before they couldn't be. And they didn't **have** to become a Jew first either. But as the scriptures say, nothing was done away with; those laws had just been fulfilled so it was time to continue on and go forward now[4].

The Church did go forward too, but only for a very short while, even though Jesus had come and established the "fullness" of his gospel and his Church upon the earth himself, people were too blind to see the truth He gave them. They rebelled against him and martyred the Apostles, as well as Him, leaving them with even less than they had to begin with. And because of the people's wickedness, He withdrew his influence from the earth, and the world fell into the "Dark Ages."

But God does not forget His people. After the Dark Ages, the gospel would have to be restored again to fulfill his plan to "*bring to pass the immortality and eternal life of man.*" But as with everything else, it would have to be done according to God's will, in His way, and in His own due time, which is not the same as ours. And that would take a while, because there would have to be that "falling away" spoken of first[5].

Then finally, the time was right. Everything was in order for His gospel to be restored again, *the final time*, in this last dispensation of the fullness of time[6], in other words, in these last days before the second coming of the Lord. It is a crucial time, when Satan's wrath and

---

4   (Matt 5:17-18) "Think not that I am come to destroy the law, or the prophets: I am not come to destroy, but to fulfil. For verily I say unto you, Till heaven and earth pass, one jot or one tittle shall in no wise pass from the law, till **all** be fulfilled."

5   (2 Thes 2:3) "Let no man deceive you by any means: for that day shall not come, except there come a falling away first"

6   (Eph 1:10) "in the dispensation of the fulness of times he might gather together in one all things in Christ"

influence will be the strongest, because he knows if he doesn't destroy God's plans and all God's children now, he will not get another chance until he must "be loosed a little season" at the end of the thousand year millennium. (Rev 20:3 "… cast him into the bottomless pit, and shut him up, and set a seal upon him, that he should deceive the nations no more, till the thousand years should be fulfilled: and after that he must be loosed a little season.)

Because this is such a critical time, God's gospel would have to be restored to its fullest, lost records would have to be reclaimed, and found, like that one I mentioned that Moses had written. There was another written by Abraham with precious information. Ezekiel tells about a book being written for the Tribe of Judah, (which of course is the Bible) as well as one written for the Tribe of Joseph, where is that? And after Jesus had been crucified and resurrected, He talked about other sheep that He needed to bring into the fold.

All the Prophets from the beginning of time, Adam, Enoch, Noah, Abraham, Moses, and others had all kept their own records and each restored the same principles and ordinances in their own dispensation of times each time after they had been lost, and added new things. So now, in these "last days," everything they had done would all have to be done again in its *entirety*, along with the special preparations needed to make things ready, and right, for the second coming of Jesus Christ, the King of this world.

It was obvious a new Prophet would have to be called especially for this "last dispensation of time" to do that work. One without any prejudices, who would be guided only by God to do the work that needed to be done. He had to be led by the spirit of revelation, as all the Prophets before him had been, and those records that had been saved for the coming forth in these last days had to be recovered.

When he obtained them, he had to be able, through the power of God, to translate them directly into our language to correct wrong interpretations and false beliefs that mankind, under the influence of Satan, had fostered. All these things, along with God's guidance would bring "light" (knowledge) back into the world. And like each time of restoration in the past, true principles and lost ordinances would have to be reintroduced, along with new truths added that we need to know to return to live with our Father in Heaven.

Unless you seek the "spirit of God" to be with you, you may have difficulty believing all these things, that God even exists, or that He can do marvelous things we don't comprehend, but Satan believes, and he will try his best to convince you of all his lies so he can drag you down to Hell right along with him if we don't believe God and understand what is going on.

It is up to you; what do you want to do or believe, or do you even want to find out for yourself what is true. Pray about this, sincerely ask to receive for yourself the ability to know the truth of these things – then you will know if it is true. I testify to the world that these things are true, they can be found out by all people that have a desire to know and understand God – who is greater, wiser, more knowledgeable and perfect than all mankind can understand, and can do marvelous works that we can't begin to comprehend.

The world didn't just happen, you weren't hatched from an ameba or protozoa, Jesus Christ **was** resurrected from the dead and rose again, and you **will** be resurrected as well. Where do you want to end up when you die? In glory **with** God; or in some lesser kingdom knowing you could have had better.

6-Aug-2009

CONCLUSION

There are so many things yet to learn. There is no conclusion to what all we can still learn in this world, or in the world to come. Any conclusion we can get here is only until the end of this mortal life. But that is only for our bodies. Our spirits will live on forever in new bodies that look much like we do (did) when we are in the prime of life. Mature, but not old or young, more like you keep trying to find in your mirror, only better – perfection.

What you get in the life after this one depends much on what you do here, so think very carefully what you are doing, and what you would like when you get to where you are going.

Then search diligently for what you need to know, to get where you want to be. The scriptures have the answers you need, to get you there. But if you leave out some of the valid scriptures, or ordinances, you will leave out something you might need and want very badly when you get there.

Ignore and fight **against** Satan, who wants to drag you down to Hell. All you will find there will be endless loneliness, misery, pain and wretchedness – in the dark and **all alone**. Would that really be what you would want for *all of eternity*? Not likely.

Instead, discover and fight *for* God the Eternal Father, and His Son Jesus Christ, who want you to ascend to the highest degree of Glory. Where there will be no end to your glory and progression, and where you will share endless love, splendor, beauty, and majesty, with your beautiful/handsome companion, and the family of God.

All that you righteously desire can be yours. You and your life will be so far beyond paradise, we don't have an adequate word to describe it.

Yes, there are other places to go in between these two extremes, but they are only stopping places where there are no exits, stairways or elevators, and progression also stops. My desires are only to always continue on to the next level, endlessly. And hope to help you get there as well. Please, let's join hands and let Jesus Christ lead us home, on the path He laid, to that glorious never ending eternity.

I hope that everyone who reads these papers will find nuggets of gold that will enrich their lives. That their faith and testimony, in the truthfulness and understanding of God, the Eternal Father, and His Son, Jesus Christ, will become so real that it will equal that of Jōb, in the land of Uz (See the story of Jōb in the Old Testament), and will never sway from that faithful stand, no matter what hardships may come.

This is my prayer, in the name of Jesus Christ, amen.